WOMEN IN
A Feminist List
Jo Campling

editorial advisory group

Maria Brenton, *University College, Cardiff*; Phillida Bunckle, *Victoria University, Wellington, New Zealand*; Miriam David, *Polytechnic of the South Bank*; Leonore Davidoff, *University of Essex*; Janet Finch, *University of Lancaster*; Jalna Hanmer, *University of Bradford*; Beverley Kingston, *University of New South Wales, Australia*; Hilary Land, *University of Bristol*; Diana Leonard, *University of London Institute of Education*; Susan Lonsdale, *Polytechnic of the South Bank*; Jean O'Barr, *Duke University, North Carolina, USA*; Arlene Tigar McLaren, *Simon Fraser University, British Columbia, Canada*; Jill Roe, *Macquarie University, Australia*; Hilary Rose, *University of Bradford*; Susan Sellers, *Centre D'Etudes Féminines, Université de Paris*; Pat Thane, *Goldsmiths' College, University of London*; Jane Thompson, *University of Southampton*; Clare Ungerson, *University of Kent at Canterbury*; Judy Walkowitz, *Rutgers University, New Jersey, USA*.

The 1970s and 1980s have seen an explosion of publishing by, about and for women. This new list is designed to make a particular contribution to this process by commissioning and publishing books which consolidate and advance feminist research and debate in key areas in a form suitable for students, academics and researchers but also accessible to a broader general readership.

As far as possible books will adopt an international perspective incorporating comparative material from a range of countries where this is illuminating. Above all they will be interdisciplinary, aiming to put women's studies and feminist discussion firmly on the agenda in subject-areas as disparate as law, physical education, art and social policy.

WOMEN IN SOCIETY
A Feminist List edited by
Jo Campling

Published

Sheila Allen and Carol Wolkowitz   **Homeworking: myths and realities**
Jenny Beale   **Women in Ireland: voices of change**
Angela Coyle and Jane Skinner (*editors*)   **Women and Work: positive action for change**
Gillian Dalley   **Ideologies of Caring: rethinking community and collectivism**
Leonore Davidoff and Belinda Westover (*editors*)   **Our Work, Our Lives, Our Words: women's history and women's work**
Diana Gittins   **The Family in Question: changing households and familiar ideologies**
Frances Heidensohn   **Women and Crime**
Muthoni Likimani (*Introductory Essay by Jean O'Barr*)   **Passbook Number F.47927: women and Mau Mau in Kenya**
Jo Little, Linda Peake and Pat Richardson (*editors*)   **Women in Cities: gender and the urban environment**
Sharon Macdonald, Pat Holden and Shirley Ardener (*editors*)   **Images of Women in Peace and War: cross-cultural and historical perspectives**
Vicky Randall   **Women and Politics: an international perspective** (2nd edn)
Rosemary Ridd and Helen Callaway (*editors*)   **Caught Up in Conflict: women's responses to political strife**
Patricia Spallone   **Beyond Conception: the new politics of reproduction**
Clare Ungerson (*editor*)   **Women and Social Policy: a reader**

Forthcoming

Eileen Aird and Judy Lown   **Education for Autonomy: processes of change in women's education**
Niam Baker   **Happily Ever After? Women's fiction in post-war Britain**
Jennifer Breen   **Women and Fiction**
Maria Brenton   **Women and Old Age**
Joan Busfield   **Women and Mental Health**
Ruth Carter and Gill Kirkup   **Women in Engineering**
Emily Driver and Audrey Droisen (*editors*)   **Child Sexual Abuse: a feminist perspective**
Lesley Ferris   **Acting Women: images of women in theatre**
Tuula Gordon   **Feminist Mothers**
Frances Gray   **Women and Laughter**
Eileen Green, Diana Woodward and Sandra Hebron   **Women's Leisure, What Leisure?**
Jennifer Hargreaves   **Women and Sport**
Annie Hudson   **Troublesome Girls: adolescence, femininity and the state**
Ursula King   **Women and Spirituality: voices of protest and promise**
Susan Lonsdale   **Women and Disability**
Mavis Maclean   **Surviving Divorce: women's resources after separation**
Jan Pahl   **Marriage and Money**
Shelley Pennington and Belinda Westover   **A Hidden Workforce: homeworkers in England, 1850–1985**
Lesley Rimmer   **Women's Family Lives: changes and choices**
Susan Sellers   **Language and Sexual Difference: feminist writing in France**
Taking Liberties Collective   **Learning the Hard Way: women's oppression and men's education**
Jane Thompson   **Introducing Women's Studies**
Deborah Valenze   **The Other Victorian Women**
Janet Wolff   **The Art of Women**
Ann Woodhouse   **Sex, Gender and Transvestism**

Women in Cities

Gender and the urban environment

Edited by

Jo Little, Linda Peake

and

Pat Richardson

**MACMILLAN
EDUCATION**

First published 1988

Published by
MACMILLAN EDUCATION LTD
Houndmills, Basingstoke, Hampshire RG21 2XS
and London
Companies and representatives
throughout the world

Typeset by Vine & Gorfin Ltd
Exmouth, Devon

Printed in China

British Library Cataloguing in Publication Data
Women in cities: gender and the urban
environment.—(Women in society).
1. Great Britain.   Urban regions.   Women.
Social conditions.   Geographical aspects
I. Little, Jo, *1958–*   II. Peake, Linda,
1956–   III. Richardson, Pat, *1958–*
IV. Series
305.4′2′0941
ISBN 0–333–45652–1 (hardcover)
ISBN 0–333–45653–X (paperback)

Series Standing Order

If you would like to receive future titles in this series as they are
published, you can make use of our standing order facility. To place a
standing order please contact your bookseller or, in case of difficulty,
write to us at the address below with your name and address and the
name of the series. Please state with which title you wish to begin your
standing order. (If you live outside the United Kingdom we may not
have the rights for your area, in which case we will forward your order
to the publisher concerned.)

Customer Services Department, Macmillan Distribution Ltd
Houndmills, Basingstoke, Hampshire, RG21 2XS, England.

Contents

Preface

Like many other edited volumes this book has a long history; time and space were both against us in our attempts to bring it to fruition. From its initial conception to handing in the manuscript, the three editors between them have lived in nine towns and held down ten different jobs. In the early 1980s, when the original idea was mooted by members of the Women and Geography Study Group (WGSG) of writing a book on geography and gender, we soon came to the realisation that there would be far too much ground to cover in an introductory text. The decision was made to write two books instead, the first to be a general text providing an introduction to feminist geography and the second to be an associated reader. The first book, *Geography and Gender* (WGSG, 1984), raised many feminist issues in relation to contemporary geographical research, putting important ideas and concepts into an accessible form. This accomplished, various members of the group embarked on the task of putting together the second book, only to discover once again that there was a surplus of material. As a result two books have emerged, the first of these, concerned with women in the developing world, is *Geography of Gender in the Third World* (Momsen and Townsend, 1987). This book, concentrating on women in Britain, is the third to come from the WGSG, the editors and contributors all being members of the group.

The WGSG of the Institute of British Geographers (IBG) came into existence in the late 1970s in response both to the growing awareness of the treatment of gender issues in many areas of associated academic study, and with the increasing dissatisfaction with the sexist nature of geographical material and the patriarchal structures operating within the work environment. The objectives of the group reflect very closely those of this book:

(1) to encourage the study of the geographic implications of gender differentiation in society and geographic research from a feminist perspective;

(2) to encourage and facilitate the exchange of information and ideas, with reference to research and teaching in the areas outlined above.

These objectives are very similar to those of the two other official women and geography groups that exist, both in North America. These are the Women and Geography Speciality Group of the Canadian Association of Geographers, and the Committee on the Status of Women in Geography of the Association of American Geographers (AAG). The similarity of objectives can be explained not only in terms of overlapping friendships and membership between the groups, but also by the status of women in the discipline. Surveys carried out in Canada, the USA, and Britain, in 1984, 1980 and 1979 respectively, revealed, for example, that women in Canadian university geography departments constituted only 6.3 per cent of the total faculty, whilst 34 per cent of these departments had no women on their staff (see Mackenzie, 1986). The study of British university geography departments identified a similarly depressing picture. Only 7 per cent of full-time staff were women and 43 per cent of departments had no women on their full-time staff (McDowell, 1979). In the United States, comparable figures for 1980 revealed that only 9.6 per cent of the members of the AAG were women and that in 1979–80 51 per cent of university geography departments in the United States and Canada had no female faculty members (Zelinsky *et al.*, 1982). In all three countries women were overrepresented in positions at the lower end of the scale, which were more likely to be temporary or part-time in nature. These disappointingly small numbers help to explain why feminism came late to geography compared to other disciplines in the social sciences; the less women are involved in the dissemination of knowledge, the less the degree to which feminism will be incorporated into that discipline's processes of teaching and research (Hanson and Monk, 1982). But these small numbers have not led to doom and despair, and in the last five years there has been a growth in the quantity of feminist geographical material produced and in the networks through which it is disseminated. The WGSG's membership is now topping the hundred mark, with members as far afield as Australia, Saudi Arabia, Spain, Canada, France, the Netherlands and the United States.

Even more important than the production of an increasing

quantity of material has been the development and refinement of theoretical and conceptual categories within feminist geography. Initially, in the 1970s, concern was with essentially descriptive studies, underpinned by a positivist approach, which focused attention on the differences between women's and men's experiences and perceptions of space and the environment, emphasising in particular the spatial constraints experienced by women (see, for example, Ferguson, 1976; Hanson and Hanson, 1976; Loyd, 1978; Libbee and McGee, 1979; Palm, 1981). Spatial constraints were then coupled with the study of gender role constraints (see Tivers, 1977). Although this research tended towards the study of women as social beings rather than biologically determined categories, women were still viewed as household surrogates rather than as independent individuals. (See Hanson and Monk, 1982; WGSG, 1984; Zelinsky *et al.*, 1982 for critiques of these studies.) This situation arose from the adoption of existing methods and frameworks of study which could only explain women's uses and perceptions of space in terms of their 'deviation' from some male environmental norm. In turn, this led to the creation of yet another special interest field – the geography of women – in which the sexist assumptions of the ideology of gender roles were often seen as 'natural' and left unchallenged. Viewing gender roles as complementary negated the reality of gender relations (as relations of inequality in which men systematically use power – both physical and economic – to subordinate women). Only with the shift in focus from women as an object of analysis to gender as a social relation of inequality between men and women, have we been able to move on from creating a geography of women to a feminist geography.

The primary task of a feminist geography is to redefine the content, orientation and nature of geographical study to reflect both female and male concerns and values, i.e. to create a more humanising geography in which women are seen not as a 'special needs' group but as one half of the human race. This objective involves the revision of theories, concepts, methodologies and the purposes of study. Such a redefinition will provide an opportunity for women to understand and explain the world they live in from the subordinate positions they occupy within it (Peake, 1985). We consider it is only with the development of a feminist approach that the way in which women are studied will change, and women's experiences, needs and interests recognised as areas of study which will help us to further understand the role of gender divisions in environmental change and development. The contributions to this book do exactly that, specifically in relation to the urban environment in Britain.

In compiling this volume it has been the intention to reach a wide-ranging audience; the contributions address diverse issues and should be of interest to many geographers. Indeed, the book aims to generate interest both amongst established feminist researchers and amongst those who are less aware of gender issues in geography. We hope that researchers and students unfamiliar with feminist theory but familiar with the inequalities between women and men in contemporary British society will benefit from this book. If it causes any of its readers to think they would like to know more about the type of geography it proposes, its production will have been worthwhile.

JO LITTLE
LINDA PEAKE
PAT RICHARDSON

Acknowledgements

As editors we should like to thank the following without whom this book would never have reached the stage of production. We are indebted to all the contributors not only for their chapters but also for their valuable advice and comments. Thanks are also due to Steve Kennedy from Macmillan for his active promotion of the book in its early stages and to Jo Campling, the Women in Society editor, for her enthusiasm and guidance. We are especially grateful to the women who typed this book, not only for their speed and efficiency but also for their genuine interest in the project and its completion. These include Jean Simmonds at Essex Institute of Higher Education, the women of the Secretariat at Kingston Polytechnic (who do not wish to be named individually) and Joan Graham. Finally, we would like to give special thanks to the members of the Women and Geography Study Group for their support and friendship throughout the book's production.

JO LITTLE
LINDA PEAKE
PAT RICHARDSON

Notes on the Contributors

Liz Bondi has been teaching in the Department of Geography at the University of Edinburgh since 1985, including from 1987 a course on Geography and Gender. Previous to this she researched into the geography and politics of contraction in local education provision for her doctorate in Geography at Manchester University. Her research interests are concerned with educational provision, gender issues and urban politics and she is presently editing a book on education and society.

Sophie Bowlby has been a lecturer in Geography at the University of Reading since 1972. She is interested in and has published various works on feminist geography, retailing and social geography. She has been an active member of the Women and Geography Study Group since its inception.

Rachael Dixey is a senior lecturer at Trinity and All Saints College, an independent college affiliated to the University of Leeds. She teaches mainly in the areas of Health Studies and Social Policy. She has lived and worked in Botswana, carrying out research into equality of access to schooling (the subject of her Ph.D. thesis), and has also worked in Papua New Guinea on a similar project. Since 1980, she has carried out research into 'women and leisure' and particularly into bingo.

Jo Little is a lecturer in Environmental Planning at Essex Institute of Higher Education in Chelmsford. Since completing her Ph.D. at Reading University, in 1984, she has worked on two major research projects (St David's College, Lampeter and University College London), both in rural geography. She has been an active member of the Women and Geography Study Group since 1982 and was joint secretary between 1985 and 1986. She has published articles on both rural and feminist geography and is at present combining the two interests in the study of women's employment opportunities in rural areas.

Suzanne Mackenzie is currently a lecturer in Geography at Carleton University in Ottawa, Canada. Her chapter is based on the research undertaken for her D.Phil. which she did at the University of Sussex and which will soon be published as a book. Her current research is concerned with the development of household–community survival strategies in de-industrialised areas of Canada.

Linda Peake is a lecturer in the School of Geography at Kingston Polytechnic. She has been an active member of the Women and Geography Study Group since the early 1980s and has published various works on feminist geography. Her interests concern research into gender and urban politics both in Britain and in the developing world, and she has recently co-edited a book on women and housing in the Third World.

Laurie Pickup has been researching into social issues in transport since 1975, particularly women's travel issues. He worked at the Transport and Road Research Laboratory for eight years and is currently employed at the Transport Studies Unit, Oxford University, where he is engaged in projects for a variety of customers concerned with transport and social issues. Since 1981 he has undertaken a considerable amount of cross-national research on commuting issues for the European Community, specialising in the impact of travel on lifestyle, working behaviour, health and safety. This research includes assessment of the international position regarding women's travel mobility to supplement his own research in the United Kingdom.

Pat Richardson is currently working at an enterprise trust in Bathgate, Scotland. She has a doctorate in Planning from the University of Reading for which she carried out research into government economic initiatives in the major English inner cities. Since 1984 she has worked in local enterprise development in London and now in Bathgate. She has been active in various women's groups since the late 1970s. Her interest in feminist geography began in 1981 when she joined the Women and Geography Study Group. She is interested in women's employment, in particular women's role in various forms of self-employment.

Jacqueline Tivers has a doctorate in Geography from the University of London and has worked as a lecturer at the University of Surrey since 1980. Since 1984 she has been a lecturer in Educational Studies, which involves organising and teaching university extramural courses in Geography and Women's Studies throughout Surrey and providing in-service training for geography teachers in schools. Her current research interests include adult education, women's education, and leisure and recreation studies.

1

Introduction: geography and gender in the urban environment

JO LITTLE, LINDA PEAKE and PAT RICHARDSON[1]

Introduction

If this book had been published a decade ago it would no doubt have started with the assertion that women have largely been absent from studies of urban life. In recent years, however, the growing interest in the activities and experiences of women has transformed this statement into something of a truism. There is now a growing body of writing on feminist issues relating to gender and the urban environment to which geographers have contributed alongside sociologists, historians, planners, architects, anthropologists, policy analysts and environmental psychologists. (See, for example, *Antipode*, 1984; Built Environment, 1984; Matrix, 1984; WGSG, 1984.) The aim of this book is to elaborate the particular contribution that feminist geography can make to the analysis of women's activities and experience and the nature of their oppression in urban areas, and to indicate the kind of research agenda to which it gives rise.

The central concerns of geography can be summarised as the relationship between society and the environment; the relationship between society and space; and the uniqueness and interdependence of place (Massey, 1984b). It is the interaction of these three concerns with an analysis of gender divisions that forms the focus of feminist geographical analysis. Feminist geography can be defined as the examination of the ways in which socio-economic, political and environmental processes create, reproduce and transform not only the places in which we live, but also the social relations between men and women in these places and how, in turn, gender relations also have an impact on these processes and their manifestations. That is, feminist geography is concerned with understanding the interrelations between socially constructed gender relations and socially constructed environments. In twentieth-century Britain, for example, we have witnessed not only a social separation, but also a spatial separation between home and work, domestic and waged labour, public and private spheres, and, increasingly, between the daily activity patterns of men and women. But the nature, manifestation and impact of these spatial separations varies over the national space economy, producing reciprocal variations in the form and content of local gender relations. Thus, we expect gender relations to vary from place to place and between environments: gender relations are constructed not only in socially and historically specific ways, but also in spatially specific settings.

The Women and Geography Study Group (WGSG) recognises four existing areas of feminist research on urban issues: the historical development of cities, particularly during the Industrial Revolution; women's impact, both through planning and political action, on urban design; speculations on a non-sexist city; and the gendered use of space in urban areas (WGSG, 1984). It is to this latter theme that this book contributes, providing theoretical and empirical studies of women's access to urban services, women's changing activity patterns in time and space, and women and men's different uses and perceptions of the urban environment. To summarise, the particular contribution of this book to the literature on women in urban environments is to illustrate that an understanding of the nature of women's oppression is greatly enhanced by examining how women's lives and activity patterns – that is, their active use of space and time – affect, and are affected by, spatial structure and environmental change.

The purpose of this editorial introduction is to provide a political and conceptual context for the chapters that follow. Within this context the book has three specific and related objectives. First, it sets out to challenge the continuing practice in geography of studying 'man' and the environment. The often unquestioned (and often unrecognised) androcentric principle (that projects a male-orientated view of society as the norm) is evident in the

empirical content, theoretical concepts and methodologies considered relevant for teaching and research. It is a common weakness
of empirical work, and it permeates the frameworks through which
the social world is studied. Monk and Hanson (1982) recognise four
areas in which the content of geographical study has a sexist bias: in
the construction of gender-blind theory; in the assumption that
people adopt traditional gender roles; in the avoidance of research
that directly addresses women's lives; and in the denial of the
significance of gender or of women's activities. These sexist biases
cannot be transformed until we alter the purpose of geographical
study and create a humanising geography that recognises the
different – sometimes reciprocal, sometimes divergent – creativity
of both genders that combine to form the human element of
human-environmental relations.

Progress towards a human-orientated geography has been slow.
Therefore, the second objective of this book is to communicate
ideas that will increase the pace of its adoption, by providing a
channel for the dissemination of both empirical and theoretical
studies of gender divisions and socially created environments.
These studies are important, not because they provide answers to
certain questions, but because they raise questions which focus
attention on the need to incorporate gender issues into the
discipline as a whole.

Implicit in these two objectives is a third, that of revealing the
relevance of feminist perspectives in the study of the urban
environment. In the individual contributions to this book a common
theme dominates, namely, that gender divisions cannot be analysed
without considering their impact on the socio-spatial organisation
of urban areas and the reciprocal way in which spatial structure
and environmental change reinforces and reflects gender relations.
As the WGSG (1984, p. 45) asserted:

> . . . feminist geographers are currently attempting to understand
> the basis for, and consequences of, the separation of 'male' and
> 'female' spheres in cities, the division of 'public' activities from
> 'private' activities, and to place an analysis of the changing
> relationship between domestic and waged labour at the centre of
> feminist urban theory.

Accordingly, this book produces material that challenges the patriarchal nature of academic life by revealing to colleagues and students the relevance of their daily lives to the academic study of geography, encouraging them to challenge conventional notions of what the study of geography is about.

The purpose of a feminist perspective in geography

Just as there are numerous theoretical approaches within geography – Marxist, neo-Marxist, positivist, realist, phenomenological, etc. – so there are a number of feminist theoretical stances – socialist, radical, new right etc. (See WGSG, 1984 for an outline of the various feminist approaches adopted in geography.) In explaining the purpose underlying the adoption of a feminist perspective, the intention here, however, is not to promote any one particular feminist perspective: women do not all live the same lives by virtue of being women. Rather the aim is to stress the unity of purpose of different feminist approaches which, unlike non-feminist approaches, share the overriding objective of understanding and improving the position of women in society. We focus in particular on the need (1) to illustrate the importance of integrating theoretical analysis with political practice; (2) to discuss topics and themes that have a significance for women's experience and understanding of everyday life; (3) and to increase awareness, both amongst geographers and non-geographers, of the significance of women's oppression in analyses of social and environmental change in urban areas.

(1)   The relationship between theoretical analysis and political practice

Implicit in the adoption of a feminist approach is a commitment to changing the conditions and context of women's daily lives. Accordingly, a major theme uniting the various feminist approaches in geography is the need to integrate theoretical analysis and political practice. Without such integration, strategies for change may be misdirected and arguments quickly become sterile. Adopting a theoretical stance, therefore, is not only necessary as an adjunct of academic enquiry, but also as an imperative of feminist practice. The relationship between theory and practice is exemplified in the academic world by the analytical tools that feminism provides to help us understand and change the position of women (not only within academia but also in society at large), and in challenging the conventional notions of what the study of geography is about.

Women in higher education occupy a subordinate position. At the same time as we struggle to change this, we are also aware of our élitist position, by virtue of being in an environment dominated by white middle-class people. But we have to view this position in its historical context: access to higher education for women has been hard won, and is still partial and divided by class and race. In the past and, sadly, in the present economic climate, equality of education for women is a myth. But if we are to change this situation then one way forward is to use the process of research and the dissemination of feminist ideas, as a mechanism of social change, which may eventually contribute to the transformation of the familiar pyramidal gender structure within academia – a substantial proportion of women at the lower end of the scale and a very small proportion at the top. (Attempting to improve the position of women in academia may, at first, seem a misplaced cause, but we firmly believe that struggling to change its power base is a part of the feminist struggle to achieve a just and equitable society devoid of sexual oppression.)

The small number of women in the discipline (see Preface) helps explain why gender issues have largely been ignored in academic study. Knowledge is a social creation, and because men dominate academia their ideas and their ways of viewing the world have become 'encoded' in knowledge and are presented as 'the' truth (Spender, 1982). Feminists have been attempting to transform this situation by exerting their influence over the production of knowledge. Rejecting the distinction between objective and subjective as a false separation that arises from a masculine experience of the world (Currie and Kazi, 1987), feminists have emphasised different ways of knowing and learning about the world by stressing the role of subjectivity in the production and validation of knowledge. Once the experiences of women are accepted as valid elements of this process, new truths and different visions of an alternative society become possible.

In academic study this process involves the acceptance of both social and self-knowledge as legitimate forms of understanding. This is not to imply that all feminists agree on the mode of production of knowledge. The feminist debate on the nature of theory is varied and complex (see Eisenstein, 1984), ranging from a concentration on 'conventional' theory i.e. the logical arrangement of facts and ideas (see, for example, Barrett, 1980) to an acceptance of women's experience as the only basis of a valid form of knowledge (see, for example, Stanley and Wise, 1983). The stance taken here is that theory needs to be accessible and practical, based on women's experience, but at the same time able to provide an overview of the diverse forms of women's oppression. As Currie and Kazi (1987, p. 93) assert:

We need research which is a way both of understanding our oppression and of bringing change. Thus the development of research which is not just 'personal' but which relates the personal to the social is a prerequisite for the unity of theory and practice. And it is by the union of theory and practice that substantial social change can be effected. Within this requirement we argue for the development of research which specifically bridges the gap between women and scholars, researchers and researched, subjects and objects. This, we think, is possible for two reasons. First, as women we can relate our personal experience to social reality; secondly, belonging to one of the oppressed groups, we can benefit from our experiential knowledge.

Feminism is not only a necessary tool to enable us to restructure our conception of the purpose of a social knowledge for women; it is also the means by which we can challenge the false separations imposed by the androcentric principle of reality. The separation of apparent opposites in our lives (of rationality and sexuality, objectivity and subjectivity, logic and emotion) has atomised our understanding of the way in which we live our daily lives, and ultimately has become equated with 'common sense'. Feminists are challenging this notion of common sense by finding new ways of understanding society and our daily lives within it. Feminists in academia can contribute to this process by presenting a fundamental challenge to the existing patriarchal control over the production of knowledge (Peake, 1985). This entails contesting four separate areas: the sex distribution of students and staff, the topics of study, theoretical concepts, and methodologies (see Mies, 1979). Transforming these four areas will help us not only to gain control over the production of knowledge in academia, but also to work collectively towards ending the oppression of women (Duelli-Klein, 1983). Feminist academic practice, then, not only introduces new ways of working within academia, but also challenges the purpose of geographical study by generating new knowledge and seeking to promote a paradigm shift within the discipline towards a more humanising human geography.

(2) *Women's experience and understanding of everyday life*

Clearly, the development of a feminist consciousness is essential if the basis of our everyday knowledge as women is to be explored and be seen as both a legitimate form of knowledge and a valid subject of study. Just as the integration of theory and practice transforms traditional academia study, asking new questions about theory and concepts also opens up new areas of empirical study. All too often colleagues have referred to feminist geography as esoteric and irrelevant, a step in the wrong direction and a waste of resources. All too often students turn off at the mention of women in their lectures. And yet if one of the major planks of geography is an understanding of the relationship between society and the environment, then an appreciation of gender differentiation is an essential element of this understanding. Why is this? Simply because women's daily lives are qualitatively different from men's, i.e. women and men perceive and use their environments differently.

The adoption of a feminist perspective opens up a new area of study, then, by allowing us to answer those questions that have arisen from women themselves and to see women not as the object of enquiry but as one of its central subjects. The lives of women do not fit into neat nine-to-five categories. The 'mundane' and 'trivial' aspects of their lives, devoted to the maintenance and reproduction of human life, often appear only at the interstices of men's activities. For example, a women gets up at 7 a.m. each day, makes breakfast for herself and two children, sees them both off to their different school bus-stops and then heads off in a third direction (all by foot) to her waged job, in a children's nursery. The children come to the nursery on their way back from school. They go home together and she makes the tea, does the washing up and helps the children with their homework. Saturdays comprise taking the weekly wash (on the back of a pushchair) to the local wash house and from there its back to the house and off again to the nearest supermarket – taking a bus there and a taxi back. Sunday is spent doing all the other jobs that need doing. Another woman also gets up at 7 a.m. each day – dresses her two youngest children and makes sure the other one gets out of bed. She makes breakfast for them all, drops off the two youngest children at the child minder's and then goes on, by car, to her job in a college of further education. She usually leaves around 4 p.m., picks up the children from the child minders', sometimes picks up others too and drops them off home. She then prepares the tea for them all, helps the eldest with his homework, puts the younger ones to bed, and does the daily wash. After that she usually has some college work to do. Her husband, working in another town, joins her for weekends.

Whilst not denying that a small but increasing number of men may lead similar lives, the reality is that these two synopses would be immediately recognised as being representative of women's lives. Of these two women, one has a car, the other does not; one has a washing machine, the other does not; one has a weekend-husband, the other has been deserted; one is white, the other black; both have waged jobs and both have children. What is common to both these women, and to millions of others, is the complexity of their daily routines and the way in which they manage, often only just, to accommodate and reconcile their patterns of activities over time and space.

From the experiences of the vast majority of women, who are engaged in both productive and reproductive activities, feminists have begun to formulate a new understanding of social change. Changes in the ownership of the means of production whilst necessary are viewed as insufficient for a totalistic understanding of social change leading to a transformation of social formations and their constituent social relations. In effect, gender-based activities are redrawing the boundaries of social change by bringing to the forefront a recognition that our relationships with other people and our concomitant activity patterns are not marginal but central to the struggle for social change. The subject matter covered in this book is, therefore, extremely relevant to the real world of social struggle.

Linked to *what* we see as important is *how* we know this to be so. Analysis of women's subordination, using both social and self-knowledge, has been put forward as the central tenet of a feminist methodology. However, placing too much emphasis on female subordination can lead to playing down female initiatives and achievements. Not only must the categories and modes of thought imposed upon society through male domination be overturned, but also we need to develop a sense of women as an active force rather than as passive or marginal beings. In the following section we outline how this can be achieved: by recognising the changing nature of the relationship between gender and the environment and examining the ways in which women themselves are organising to satisfy the needs arising from their gendered roles.

(3) Gender oppression in analyses of social and environmental change

The adoption of a feminist perspective enables the underlying causes of women's oppression and the mechanisms by which it is perpetuated to be studied both theoretically and empirically. Analyses of topics such as the sexual division of labour, the ideology underlying the nuclear family, women's dual roles, the public and private spheres, women's roles in production and reproduction, gender-role differentiation and men's control of knowledge and sexuality, have all served to increase our understanding of women's oppression (see, for example, Barrett, 1980; Spender, 1982; Segal, 1987). These issues are particularly important to the study of geography because they enhance understanding of the ways in which women's activities are changing over time and space and the effect such transformations are having on the environment and upon the construction of the gender categories 'women' and 'men' i.e. what it means to be 'human'.

As Mackenzie (1988) argues the gender category 'women' has been changing over time as women's activity patterns have changed. As women have campaigned for birth control, better housing and jobs, the nature of their waged and domestic labour has been transformed causing reciprocal ideological changes of emphasis in the attributes of 'women', from that of 'mother' in the post-war period, to that of 'mother and part-time worker' in the 1960s and 1970s to 'mother' again in the 1980s. Yet the reality in Britain in the 1980s is that only a small minority of women play out this one and only role of 'mother'. Many women have dual roles, as mothers and waged workers. Whether they live with their spouses or with relatives or alone as one-person households, their increasing demands for better housing, better child-care facilities, better transportation and alternative living arrangements reveal that the environment within which women live fails to recognise their needs.

These changes in women's roles in the post-war period and women's responses to them, manifestations both of trans-formations in gender relations, are changing the geography of everyday life. By revealing the importance of gender relations in everyday activities over time and space, a feminist analysis challenges geography 'to examine how the environments we create reflect or relate to gender relations and how, in turn, those environments reinforce or (re-) create existing or new forms of gender relations' (McDowell and Bowlby, 1983, p. 97). Why has gender increasingly come to be identified as a significant parameter of environmental change? Several factors have been identified as being of importance (Bowlby, Foord and McDowell, 1986). First, within the post-war period in Britain there has been the growth of the Women's Liberation Movement which made women as a social group more visible. Secondly, within the same period there have been major social and economic changes in women's lives, for example, the increase in the number of women entering the formal labour market, especially in part-time work and by women from ethnic minorities, the increase in women's unemployment and the growth of informal sector work by women in the home and the com-munity. Thirdly, and more recently, theoretical stances have devel-oped within academic geography, such as humanism and realism, which are more sensitive to issues of gender. There has also been the development, within recent locality studies, of theoretical and conceptual frameworks which have recognised that although the uniqueness of places has largely been attributed to international and national transformations in economic organisation and social relations, no less important in shaping the particularity of places are the variations in local patriarchal relations between women and men. Finally, it was with the (albeit small) increase in the number of women geographers studying transformations in urban and regional structure since the early 1970s that the need to extend existing patterns of environmental and spatial change to take account of gender divisions came to be recognised.

Over time feminist geographical study has developed from its initial concern with critiques of the invisibility of women in the environment (Hayford, 1974) to concentrate on two themes: first, issues of particular concern to women as a 'special needs' group, such as domestic labour and child care, within which women were treated as 'household surrogates' (Tivers, 1978); and secondly, critiques of models of urban structure that assumed society was composed of nuclear families with traditional sexual divisions of labour. A major criticism of these models was that, 'by failing to examine, for example, the effect of women's growing labour force participation and changes in family patterns on income distribution in the city, shopping, journey to work, residential patterns, and needs for specific social services, planning policies potentially exacerbated difficulties faced by urban residents, especially those faced by women whose lives no longer conformed to the "traditional pattern"' (Mackenzie, 1984, p. 5). To compensate for this deficiency, feminist geographers began to document aspects of women's lives in relation to their spatial activities in the city, focusing in particular on spatial constraints (Hanson and Hanson, 1976; Palm and Pred, 1974; Rengert, 1975; Tivers, 1977; Zelinsky *et al.*, 1982) or on the way in which the division of labour between men and women resulted in specific spatial forms. For example, at the micro scale the gendered division of space resulted in the home interior being assigned to women and the exterior – the garden, the garage – to men. At the city-scale men were seen to appropriate the public arenas of the city centres, whilst women were supposedly confined to the interpersonal private sphere of the suburbs where they carried out their reproductive tasks within the confines of the family and local community.

The underlying thread tying this work together was that of gender roles. However, the studies conducted tended to see gender roles as static and fixed constraints: women's roles were environmentally determined. A framework was needed which would enable understanding of the way in which gender roles were constructed and how women actively participated in accepting or rejecting new gender identities. Rather than emphasise constraints, viewing spatial restrictions as causal entities, there was a need for a fuller understanding of the structuring of space as the outcome of a social process in which people actively participated in creating social structures and practices (Foord and Gregson, 1986). The approach adopted has been to see the gender category 'women' not as a fixed historical entity, but as one structured by the social relations between men and women, which in turn leads to the formation of the gendered identities of women and men. Thus, rather than women's subordination being 'explained' through the daily roles played out by women and men, the focus has moved on to gender relations – the social conceptions of masculinity and femininity – with the concomitant understanding that as gender relations change so does the way in which men and women create, reproduce and change the environments in which they live. In turn the environment and its transformation, reflects, reproduces and alters gender relations.

The separation of home and work and the development of city suburbs clearly demonstrates this reciprocal relationship. The post-war expansion of residential areas beyond the city centre (in both Britain and North America) was not simply a spatial process, but held profound implications for the social and economic organisation of individual households and for the operation of gender relations. As Mackenzie (1986) argues, daily life in early twentieth-century suburbia revolved around very clearly defined behaviour patterns amongst men and women: men travelled into the city centre to work in order to provide the household with an income, while women stayed at home performing the domestic duties – the reproductive activity which made it possible for men to go out to work.

> The standard pattern of urban-suburban development was thus built upon a set of gender roles, and reinforced these. Women animated the home and community, pulling together all the activities which went on there. In so doing, they became 'naturally' associated with these activities and their attendant values. These activities and values came to be seen as the constituents of women's nature, just as financial rationality and public responsibility came to be seen as the constituents of men's nature. (Mackenzie, 1986, p. 4)

More recently, particularly since the 1960s, growing numbers of married women have been taking on waged work. While in 1931, for example, only 4 per cent of the total workforce comprised married women, by 1981 this had risen by over six times to 26 per cent (WGSG, 1984, p. 69). This entry by married women into the labour market has not, however, been accompanied by any general renegotiation of their domestic role. Women still retain responsibility for the reproductive duties within the household, the cooking, cleaning and child care. Thus women who do undertake waged work are generally carrying the burden of a dual role. The spatial separation of different functions within the city imposes severe constraints on the activity patterns of these women, in relation to both aspects of their lives, home and work, and consequently reinforces their dual role

Feminist geographers are also attempting to demonstrate that the environmental and spatial forms created by social, economic and political processes affect different groups of women in varying ways. Specific studies have taken account of groups of women such as housewives (Tivers, 1985), elderly women (Helms, 1974), female criminals (Rengert, 1975), homeless women (Stapleton-Concorde, 1986), women in the Third World (Monsen and Townsend, 1987), middle-class women (Miller 1983), unemployed women (Walby, 1983), black women (Davies and Fowler, 1971), prostitutes (Rubin, 1975), and single-parent mothers (Klodawsky, Aron and Rose, 1985). However, the vast majority of work has focused on women as a homogenous social group either in waged work or involved in home-based activities. But investigation must go further so that it takes account of the interrelations between gender, life-cycle, class, ethnicity and culture. This book goes some way towards correcting this situation; the chapter by Rachael Dixey focuses solely on working-class women, whilst those by Sophie Bowlby and Suzanne Mackenzie examine specific experiences of women differentiated by class and Liz Bondi and Linda Peake discuss the relationship between gender and ethnicity. As feminists we are aware of the double oppression suffered by women from ethnic minorities. The combination of oppression based on both gender *and* race has resulted in ethnic minority women being at the bottom of the pile, whether in terms of access to jobs, wage levels, working conditions, welfare, health care, housing, education, transport and all the other daily necessities of life. As geographers, however, we have not yet started to examine the interactions between gender and race, and yet there are serious questions to be asked of the nature of the relationship between patriarchy, racism and imperialism, not least in connection with the spatial strategies employed by these processes to keep ethnic minority women in a subordinate position. As geographers we have a history of experience concerned with the nature of environmental and social change. To this we need to add our knowledge as feminist academics to reveal that women's activity patterns are an important aspect of social organisation of the urban environment.

Individual contributions

Having outlined the aims of the book and considered its broad objectives within the context of the purpose of a feminist perspective in geography, attention now turns to the chapters themselves and to the major themes they incorporate. The structure of the book reflects one of its major objectives, namely, to provide a framework for the bringing together of theoretical and empirical research in feminist geography. There are two main theoretical chapters confronting many of the key issues concerning gender and the urban environment, followed by four empirically based studies relating to various aspects of women's lives in urban environments. The theory chapters, by Liz Bondi and Linda Peake (Chapter 2) and Suzanne Mackenzie (Chapter 3), focus specifically on urban politics and aspects of the spatial and temporal organisation of the city. Together they act as an essential springboard for the remaining four chapters all of which are based on original research. The topics covered are wide ranging: Sophie Bowlby examines retailing (Chapter 4); Jacqueline Tivers explores the constraints operating on women with young children (Chapter 5); Laurie Pickup investigates accessibility and women's mobility (Chapter 6); and, finally, Rachael Dixey examines aspects of women's leisure activities (Chapter 7). These four empirical chapters concentrate largely on the roles women perform, describing how their activities are constrained both by aspects of their domestic work and by the sexual division of labour. Unlike many early studies in geography, however, which sought simply to treat women as another special interest group, these contributions recognise the importance of looking beyond gender roles in an attempt to explain women's subordination. All contributors agree that along with class and ethnic divisions, women's position in society is largely a function of the underlying power structures that exist between men and women and a fuller understanding of such power structures is necessary to be able to analyse women's subordinate position. Thus, while the examination of gender roles can provide very important evidence of the experiences of women this evidence must be seen in the light of the broader theoretical issues raised in Chapters 2 and 3, and discussed below.

First, in the study of gender and the urban environment, one of the major directions developed by geographers concerns the spatial division between different functions in the city. The problems encountered by women, as a result of the physical separation of different functions of the city, constitute an important theme for all chapters in this book. For Tivers and Pickup, this separation provides a central focus. These authors demonstrate both the difficulties of access which women experience in relation to many service functions and to employment, and the mobility constraints which result from such difficulties. Mobility constraints occur not simply as a result of deficiencies in public and private transport provision, but also through the difficulties of coping with young children and from a fear of violence and sexual harassment. Bowlby and Dixey also recognise the implications of the spatial separation of different activities within urban areas. Bowlby considers the changing location of retailing functions, emphasising specifically the reduction in the number of local outlets with the increasing spatial concentration of facilities, usually in out-of-town locations. Finally, Dixey notes the constraints imposed on working-class women's leisure activities. She draws attention to the lack of choice available to working-class women in terms of both the type and location of leisure activities, and suggests that this lack of choice is one of the major reasons for the popularity of bingo amongst these women.

With varying degrees of emphasis, all authors draw attention to the importance of the more specific spatial separation of home and work in reinforcing women's subordinate position in the domestic sphere. Not only does this separation, coupled with problems of mobility, act to restrict women's employment opportunities, but it extends the time required for them to perform their domestic work. Furthermore, current cutbacks in public service provision and the centralisation of facilities further perpetuate established gender roles.

In both feminist and non-feminist literature the separation of physical spaces within the city has been reflected, at an analytical level, in the division between 'production' and 'reproduction'; production representing (so called) real work in the creation of goods for exchange, and reproduction, the 'secondary' activity of servicing the needs of the household and of those engaged in productive work. The production/reproduction division is one which features significantly in each of the chapters. Bondi and Peake, who discuss the conceptualisation of 'production' and 'reproduction' within the field of urban politics, argue that existing work in this area has promoted too rigid a separation of the two spheres, viewing them as analytically discrete rather than as 'two sides of the same coin'. This work, they contend, has maintained a highly simplistic interpretation of reproduction which rarely extends beyond the reproduction of labour power. The emphasis, within this debate, on collective rather than individual consumption, has ignored the significance of the domestic sphere and of work undertaken in the 'private' sphere of the home and family. This debate is taken up by Mackenzie in her chapter. Drawing attention again to the inadequacies of common conceptualisations of production and reproduction, she considers their shifting boundaries within the city. Demonstrating that just as the processes of 'production' and 'reproduction' cannot be regarded as discrete and unchanging, so do the spheres in which these activities take place, interact and overlap. Particular emphasis is given to the way in which women themselves can influence the physical and social environment of urban areas (particularly the relationship between work and home) by gaining control of their own fertility and childbirth and extending this control to child care.

All four empirical chapters provide examples of the ways in which domestic work is undervalued. As women are primarily, and often exclusively, responsible for domestic tasks within the household, the lack of value attributed to domestic work has particular implications for them. Caring for children, shopping, meal preparation, cleaning, etc. are all viewed within society as non-stressful, simple tasks which can be quickly and easily undertaken by women leaving them free for much of the day to engage in paid employment or leisure activities. But as shown by the contributors to this book, women's domestic work, rather than freeing them to engage in other activities, particularly leisure and paid employment, actually constrains their activities in these spheres. Dixey illustrates the way in which women are forced to 'choose' those leisure activities which have a considerable degree of flexibility and can be arranged around their domestic responsibilities. For this reason, she suggests, bingo is a popular and well-supported activity amongst certain groups of women. Similarly, Tivers and Pickup note how the responsibilities of child care, particularly in terms of escorting children to and from school and looking after them during school holidays, prevents many women from seeking employment beyond their immediate locality, despite the potentially greater financial and personal benefits of doing so.

Another dichotomy that has been important in the analysis of gender issues in the city is that of the 'public' and the 'private'. As with production and reproduction, geographers have sought, in rather simplistic fashion, to map this analytical dichotomy onto distinct spatial sectors of the city and to treat these sectors as separate and unchanging. Thus, the 'public' has been equated with the market place and affairs of state, while the 'private' has been associated with the home, the family and interpersonal relations. In the study of gender and the urban environment, it has commonly been suggested that women are restricted to the private sphere and that access to the public world is largely limited to men. More recently, however, the inadequacies of this division have been recognised (see Imray and Middleton, 1983; McDowell, 1983); Garmarnikow and Purvis (1983), for example, suggest that its past academic use has imposed a conceptual strait-jacket on the analysis of society. Greater consideration, it is now maintained, must be given, as in the treatment of production and reproduction, to the interaction and interconnectivity of the two spheres.

Criticism of the use of the public–private dichotomy is developed in the theoretical chapters in this collection. Bondi and Peake argue that the separation of the spheres has allowed 'personal' issues such as child care and domestic relations to be divorced from the public arena and be relegated to the private world. Consequently, issues surrounding individual, as opposed to collective, consumption, many of which concern women rather than men, are given little public recognition and command a low political profile. Mackenzie is also concerned with the transformations occurring, within the city, in the relationship between, and distribution of, 'public' and 'private' spaces. The historical perspective which she adopts allows her to specify how women's organisation in cities has been both constrained by and has actively altered the public–private dichotomy. Changes in women's use of space within the city have come about, largely, as a result of women starting collectively to organise aspects of their domestic responsibilities. These changes, Mackenzie argues, have succeeded in opening up the 'private' sphere of the home to outside 'public' influences. Pickup also draws attention to these changes, examining the implications for women's travel needs of the renegotiation of the boundaries between separate spheres.

A third common theme uniting the individual chapters is women's dual role. The post-war involvement of growing numbers of women, particularly married women, in waged work in Britain has not, it is argued, been accompanied by any general renegotiation in the distribution of domestic duties within the household. In other words, women are still responsible for the majority of domestic tasks, regardless of their involvement in paid employment. Thus women are forced to accept the double burden of a dual role; as a partner and mother and as a wage earner. This dual role places severe constraints on women's activities and imposes strict limitations on their job opportunities. The need to collect children from school, care for them during school holidays and generally service the demands of the household determines the location and hours of employment for the majority of women. Consequently, the opportunities for most women either to undertake a job of their particular choice or to progress up the career ladder are minimised, despite the fact that in many cases the income from women's employment forms a crucial part of the total household income.

Tivers focuses directly on the nature and problems of women's dual role. She presents evidence of the way in which constraints that operate on women's paid employment are compounded by their domestic responsibilities, particularly caring for young children. This dual role, she demonstrates, frequently deprives women, not only of satisfactory employment, but of leisure time (an assertion which is supported by Dixey in her chapter on leisure). While the other contributors place rather less emphasis on describing the characteristics of women's dual role, they nevertheless recognise and draw attention to its importance to contemporary gender relations. Bowlby, for example, discusses the continuing involvement of women in the purchasing and preparation of food. Such involvement forms a highly important aspect of women's role, regardless of whether or not they are engaged in paid employment. As she outlines, the actual form of women's participation in shopping for and preparing food has changed over time and continues to vary between classes. Ultimately, however, in the vast majority of households, it is the woman who has and always has had final responsibility for these activities.

The final theme, common to each of the chapters, is a discussion of 'the future' and of possible changes in women's position. Pickup, for example, investigates the likelihood of alternative transport initiatives which cater specifically for women's needs becoming more widely accepted within transport policy. Bowlby, in turn, focuses on the innovations currently taking place in retailing and on the possible introduction of alternative forms of shopping such as teleshopping, and their implications for women. Bondi and Peake and Mackenzie, however, move away from specific initiatives and take a wider perspective making a number of observations concerning the changing organisation of women's lives and the future British city. In making these observations, they reassert the need for the transformation of social relations and social processes to be analysed in the context of the distribution of power between women and men.

Even from this brief discussion, the interconnectivity of the major themes within this book is clearly displayed. The underlying importance of women's domestic role and its perpetuation through the spatial and analytical separation of different functions and activities within the city is readily apparent. Moreover, all contributors have been concerned to demonstrate the changing nature of women's experience: gender roles and relations are not static and changes in patterns of employment and in the overall relationship between home and work have had profound implications for various aspects of women's lives. Thus, although all chapters discuss the experiences of women in relation to the contemporary city, thereby reinterpreting our understanding of the present, some also take a historical perspective, reinterpreting our understanding of the past. While each chapter within this volume stands alone, their articulation of common themes unites them both in the context of this book and of wider debates within feminist geography.

20   *Introduction*

Notes

1. The editors would like to thank the contributors for their remarks on
    the introduction, in particular Liz Bondi and Suzanne Mackenzie for
    their invaluable comments.

Further reading

Hamilton, R. and Barrett, M. (eds) (1986) *The Politics of Diversity:
   Feminism, Marxism and Nationalism* (London: Verso).
Matrix (1984) *Making Space: Women and the Man-Made Environment*
   (London: Pluto).
Segal, L. (1987) *Is the Future Female? Troubled Thoughts on Contempor-
   ary Feminism* (London: Virago).
Stimpson, S., Dixler, E., Nelson, M. and Yatrakis, K. (eds) (1981) *Women
   and the American City* (Chicago: University of Chicago Press).

2

Gender and the city: urban politics revisited

LIZ BONDI and LINDA PEAKE

This chapter examines the importance of gender relations in urban
politics. During the last decade, the concept 'urban' has been the
subject of extensive debate. Previously, cities had often been
classified according to the industries located within their boundaries
or hinterlands. This approach presupposed a direct connection
between local productive activities and the sustenance of the local,
urban population. However, the city is no longer the spatial unit
within which productive activities are organised: in both developed
and developing countries the organisation of industrial production
has expanded to the regional, national or international scale. In
other words, cities are embedded in, and sustained by, economic
systems that extend far beyond their boundaries. But cities remain
the places where the great majority of the populations of developed
countries, and a growing proportion of the populations of developing countries, live. This observation led the neo-Marxist theorist
Castells (1976, 1977, 1978) to advance the persuasive argument that
it is more appropriate to consider the city as the locus, or spatial unit
of the 'reproduction of labour power', than as the spatial unit of
production. Subsequent work in urban studies has been strongly
influenced by Castells' approach: the notion that processes involved
in the reproduction of labour power are the key to understanding
the structure of, and activity within, urban areas underlies much
recent research (see, for example, contributions to Harloe, 1981
and Harloe and Lebas, 1981). However, critiques of this approach
are now emerging, to which this chapter aims to contribute (also see
Klausner, 1986; Preteceille, 1986).

The term 'the reproduction of labour power' refers to the processes that enable people to return to work each day, and to be replaced from one generation to the next. These include, for example, the provision of housing and transport, domestic activities such as cooking and child care, and biological reproduction. However, although 'urban politics' was redefined by Castells as the politics of the reproduction of labour power, in practice attention has focused almost entirely upon those aspects of the reproduction of labour power that are provided, at least in part, by the state. In this chapter we argue that the omission of other aspects of 'reproduction' is closely associated with the failure of urban theorists to consider the significance of gender divisions.

Many of the processes that ensure the reproduction of labour power occur in the home or in the community rather than at the workplace, where labour becomes productive[1]. The dichotomy between home and community, on the one hand, and the workplace, on the other, carries with it notions of two spheres of social relations, the first widely characterised as female and the second widely characterised as male (Elshtain, 1981). This suggests that questions of gender are central to the notion of urban politics. However, the significance of gender relations within urban politics remains neglected (but see McDowell, 1983; Mackenzie and Rose, 1983; Wekerle, 1984). We consider this omission detrimental to an important area of study, and in this chapter develop a critique informed by feminism. Our focus (in line with other contributions to this book) is on Great Britain. In the first section, the development of urban political studies in Britain is briefly discussed. The second section considers the importance of gender divisions within the terms of reference adopted in recent studies of urban politics. These terms of reference, however, are open to criticism. Accordingly, the third section presents a feminist critique of the term 'urban'. The fourth section focuses on the term 'politics' and outlines a feminist reformulation of urban politics.

The development of urban politics in Britain

The work of Castells was central to the emergence on the Continent of a new Marxist school of urban and regional studies, in the late 1970s, which is also represented by Lojkine (1976, 1977), Lebas

(1977), Mingione (1977) and Preteceille (1981). Various 'community struggles', arising, for example, from slum clearance and urban redevelopment programmes, attracted the attention of these writers. They questioned the primacy accorded to production in classical Marxist theory, and emphasised the significance of the reproduction of labour power. Studies focused on the contribution of conflicts over state provision of services (such as housing, education, transport, health and welfare) to class-based movements committed to socialism. These academic developments were associated with changes in political organisations, most notably, the emergence of the Euro-communist movement, which sought to unify 'urban struggles' (or 'urban social movements') with the movement for socialism.

Local politics have been studied in Britain for many years, but this continental school aroused a new wave of interest in urban political theory (Dunleavy, 1979, 1980a; Saunders, 1979, 1981). Interpretations of political developments, however, cannot easily be transposed from one country to another. In Britain, as in many Western European countries, local protest over public provision, planning decisions and the like became widespread in the 1960s and 1970s (Bell and Newby, 1976; Elliott and McCrone, 1981), but the relationship between these protest movements and political parties differed geographically. In Britain, the political response of the Left has been strongly influenced by a reformist, social democratic Labour Party, generally unwilling to associate itself with extra-Parliamentary political action[2]. Consequently, urban protest movements have tended to remain isolated from the organised left and observers have focused less upon the potential unity of urban and class movements than upon evidence of their disunity (Bell and Newby, 1976; Pahl, 1977a). These empirical observations have informed critiques of Castells' work advanced by British social and political theorists (Dunleavy, 1980a; Saunders, 1981; Urry, 1981).

Saunders (1979) argued that housing generates material interests distinct from, and cutting across, interests arising from class position. That is, the access of an individual to private housing (primarily through owner-occupation) materially affects life chances in a manner analagous to, but only partially determined by, access to the means of production (capital ownership) and occupational status. Dunleavy (1979) has used the term 'consumption cleavage' to describe the distinction between social groups reliant upon public and private forms of provision. He provided empirical evidence of the influence on political alignment of differences in housing tenure (between owner-occupation and council tenancy) and differences in means of transport (between private car and public transport):

> Because consumption cleavages and their effects on political alignment are fundamentally structured by state intervention, they cross-cut occupational class lines. The implications of this are asymmetrical. The preponderance of individualized modes of consumption in the numerically smaller non-manual grades means that consumption effects overwhelmingly reinforce occupational class effects. In contrast manual workers are highly fragmented in terms of their consumption locations. The ideological and political structures accompanying consumption locations thus fundamentally weaken the links between manual workers and the Labour Party. (Ibid., p. 443)

Underlying the political consequences of different forms of provision is the post-war development of the welfare state. This resulted (at least initially) in a marked increase in the number of consumers and clients of public services. Further, the role of the state 'from the cradle to the grave' extended public intervention into all aspects of daily life (Habermas, 1976; Conference of Socialist Economists, 1980; Bleitrarch and Chenis, 1981). These interventions underlay the new forms of conflict and protest observed in the 1960s (Elliott and McCrone, 1981; Ley, 1980). Consequently, the activities of the state in the provision of services have provided an important focus of attention in urban politics, particularly at the scale of local authorities, through which many services are provided (Cockburn, 1977a; Pahl, 1977b; Saunders, 1979). The growth of the public sector also led to a great increase in state employment, and the significance of this for political alignment and community protest has also been pursued in urban political analysis (Dunleavy, 1980b). Since the late 1970s, public expenditure has been cut back and the expansion of the welfare state has been curtailed if not reversed, prompting further conflict over issues of state provision. Dunleavy (1986) suggests that political divisions arising from differential access to, and reliance upon, state services is of critical importance to the ability of right-wing governments, such as those led by Mrs Thatcher, to cultivate and retain electoral support. Thus, this body of work in urban studies continues despite changes in the political and economic context.

One important feature of these studies is that they neither insist upon the primacy of class, as in mainstream Marxist work (for example, Harloe, 1977), nor assert that class is 'withering away' as propounded by the 'post-industrialist theorists' (for example, Bell, 1973). We endorse the aim of unravelling the relationship between issues of class and socialist politics, on the one hand, and issues of 'consumption' and community or urban protests, on the other. However, existing work on urban politics suffers from several difficulties. First, within its declared aim of studying the politics of consumption, the crucial issue of gender divisions has been neglected. Secondly, this declared aim is open to criticism and we argue below that limiting the 'urban' element of urban politics to 'consumption' is incorrect. Thirdly, the 'politics' element of urban politics has also been interpreted in unduly narrow terms. The sections that follow examine each of these problems in turn.

Gender divisions and 'collective consumption'

In his earlier work, Castells was primarily concerned with 'collective consumption', that is, with state provision of goods and services (such as housing and education) necessary for the reproduction of labour power (Castells, 1976, 1977, 1978). Castells has subsequently altered his position (Castells, 1983), but until very recently, nearly all studies in urban politics drew on his earlier work, in which gender differences were recognised only in so far as the dichotomy between production and consumption reflects and is reflected by a division between male and female activities. Hence Castells' remark: 'The contemporary city . . . rests on the subordination of women consumers to male producers' (Castells, 1978, p. 178).

This conceptualisation is remarkably inadequate. Issues of consumption do have a particular salience for women, but gender roles cannot be mapped directly on to a dichotomy between production and consumption: women are neither exclusively consumers (they are also producers) nor the only consumers (men are also consumers). Moreover, there are important differences between women and between men belonging to different social, racial and ethnic groups.

To understand the importance of gender in the politics of consumption, it is necessary to examine the roles of women and men more carefully, particularly the ways in which these roles have changed in recent years. The post-war expansion of state provision was closely linked to changes in gender divisions. Between 1951 and 1971, 2.5 million jobs were created, of which 2.2 million were taken by women including, at least initially, many arriving from the West Indies and East Africa. In 1951, women accounted for 30 per cent of the workforce; by 1981 they accounted for 42 per cent. The entry of married women into the workforce was particularly important and, by 1981, 61 per cent of married women were economically active, over half working part-time (Lewis, 1984). Expansion occurred principally in the public services: the new jobs were for clerical workers, nurses, ancillary health workers, teachers, social workers and so on. The growth of female participation in waged employment itself fuelled the demand for services such as nurseries, school meals and old people's homes, while the wages earned by women stimulated the production of consumer goods and services, including convenience foods, automatic washing machines and launderettes. The entry of women into the workforce has also been associated with changes in family life. Notwithstanding demographic variations between ethnic and social groups, completed family size and the time between the last birth and a woman's return to paid employment have, on average, both decreased in recent years.[3]

These changes have not eradicated pre-existing gender divisions but have resulted in women having to organise their time between more activities. Wilson (1977a) has argued, the growth of the welfare state did not relieve women of their primary responsibility for domestic life; rather it increased the role of the state in perpetuating existing gender divisions. For example, after the Second World War, state provision for young children was almost entirely withdrawn, the chief exception being for the children of 'unfit' mothers. Despite substantial demand, state provision for pre-school age children has remained limited (see David, 1983). Social policies repeatedly presume and effectively define the 'proper' structure of family relations and women's responsibilities within the family unit. The Sex Discrimination Act of 1975 exempts statutory provisions from its portfolio, leaving the state free to discriminate against women in welfare and taxation systems, which it does by treating women, wherever possible, as wives and mothers and not as autonomous individuals (Barrett, 1980). Thus the entry of women into employment has altered but not reduced the role of women as consumers: women continue to be in the 'front line' over issues arising from the provision of services in the public and private sector, frequently on behalf of the members of their households:

> (Women are) in the front line of interaction with the local state. When someone 'has to go and see the schoolteacher about the truant child, when someone has to answer the door to the social worker, or go and face the music at the rent office: it's the woman . . . Women are also . . . in the front line of interaction with capital in its distributive guise. They are the shoppers. Apart from beer and fags the household necessities in most families are bought by women. (Cockburn, 1977b, p. 63)

Many women can aptly be described as having ' dual roles', as wage earners and as unpaid domestic workers (hence the prevalence of part-time working among women).

Moreover, the participation of women in the labour force has not been on equal terms with men. Despite the Equal Pay and Sex Discrimination Acts, women's earnings remain markedly lower than those of men: the average hourly pay of women rose slightly after the implementation of legislation in 1975, but then stabilised at approximately 75 per cent that of men. The failure of the sex equality legislation to achieve more is largely a function of gender segregation at work. Of men in the labour force, half are in jobs where the workforce is 90 per cent male; of women, half are in jobs where the workforce is 70 per cent female (Phillips, 1983). 'Women's' jobs typically involve tasks requiring supposedly female attributes such as dexterity (for component assembly in the electronics industry), docility (for routine clerical and cleaning work) and caring skills (for nursing and nursery teaching). As Lewis (1984) argues, most of these tasks are classified as unskilled or semi-skilled and most relate closely to those required for domestic work. Thus the position of women in the workforce has often served to reinforce rather than undermine traditional divisions of labour within the family.

In emphasising the significance of gender divisions at work and at home, it must not be assumed that men and women form homogeneous groups. Gender divisions exist alongside and interact with class, racial and ethnic divisions. Addressing the potential conflict experienced by women between loyalties to their sex and to their class, Phillips (1987) argues that gender divisions have been central to changing definitions and understandings of class status. Thus, in the mid nineteenth century, the position of women was fundamental to middle-class status: the occupational status or income of a man was often less significant to being middle class than the presence of a women following a genteel life with no paid work outside the home and little work at home. In the second half of the twentieth century, such class distinctions are less pronounced. However, class differences in, for example, household income and income security persist and influence the political priorities of women. This reduces the scope for unity between women (see Campbell, 1984; Pahl, 1984; Phillips, 1987).

Racial and ethnic divisions are similarly enmeshed with gender divisions (see Anthias and Yuval-Davis, 1983; Bryan *et al.*, 1985). Thus, within households, gender relations vary between racial and ethnic groups as well as between classes. For example, 31 per cent of West Indian households with children are single-parent units, compared with 10 per cent of white households and 5 per cent of Asian households (Brown, 1984), although in all cases the great majority of these households consist of a lone woman with children. Similarly, rates of economic activity vary between women of different ethnic groups: in 1981, 23 per cent of white women, 47 per cent of West Indian women and 25 per cent of Asian women were in full-time work; 17 per cent of white women, 14 per cent of West Indian women and 5 per cent of Asian women were in part-time work (OPCS, 1982a). Moreover, gender segregation at work is inseparable from racial segregation. White women are concentrated in non-manual occupations (especially clerical work and retailing); black women are concentrated in manual work, Asians particularly in the clothing trade, West Indian women in engineering and the health service (see Mama, 1984).

The onset of the current recession has further changed the position of women. Cuts in public provision affect everyone but, as Edgell and Duke (1983) have noted:

the current attack on the welfare state is predominantly an attack on women as (a) the major contributors of wage labour to collective social provision, (b) the major beneficiaries of collective social provision, and (c) the major care role providers in the family and society. (p. 375)

For example, cuts in social services involve a transfer of function from the state to the family, within which extra tasks such as care for pre-school age children and for the elderly usually fall to women. Consequently, some women have had to give up work to look after the young, the old or the infirm, while others have lost jobs as services have been cut (Edgell and Duke, 1983.)[4] Overall, job losses have been greatest in regions dominated by traditional industries such as shipbuilding and steel, which have always been male preserves. In these areas, women's employment has remained relatively buoyant (Massey, 1984a). However, women suffer disproportionately under 'last in, first out' redundancy policies and practices of dismissing part-time staff, who have least employment protection, when lay-offs are made (Lewis, 1984). Thus, between 1976 and 1981, unemployment among married women is estimated to have increased threefold (Marshall, 1982; also see Martin and Roberts, 1984, on the problem of defining unemployment among women). High rates of unemployment have been accompanied by polarisation within the workforce, between those in secure and better-paid jobs, for whom living standards have risen and those in insecure and low-paid jobs. The latter include approximately one in five male workers and two in three female workers (Bazen, 1985). Consequently, for a substantial sector of the population the resources available have declined as the demands on the family have increased.

Again, these trends have affected different groups of women to differing degrees. In terms of unemployment, among all age groups rates are higher for black men and women than for white men and women. The incidence of low pay is also greater for non-whites than whites. Nationally, it has been estimated that two-thirds of the jobs lost as a result of privatisation (for example in the National Health Service) have been women's jobs and in London between 50 per cent and 80 per cent of these had been occupied by women from ethnic minorities (Women's Equality Group, 1987; also see Bryan *et al.*, 1985). Divisions between men and women, between racial groups and between social classes have made the implementation of policies resulting in job losses easier (see Carby, 1982; Mama, 1984; Phillips, 1987).

Clearly, the relationship between gender and issues arising from public provision is complex. Shifts in provision between the state and the family (and the private sector) both have different consequences for women and men, and for different social, racial and ethnic groups. Moreover, these shifts are predicated upon particular sexual divisions, while their implementation depends also on social and racial divisions. However, little attention has been paid to gender differences as either a causal factor or an effect in studies of urban politics (but see Edgell and Duke, 1983).

Urban politics, consumption and the reproduction of labour power

Urban political studies are open to criticism not only for overlooking gender issues but also for their preoccupation with 'consumption', particularly 'collective (or socialised) consumption'. This has led to the neglect of (a) the interaction between processes of 'production' and 'reproduction', (b) certain aspects of 'reproduction', which are central to the lives of many women, and (c) subjective aspects of the processes involved in 'reproduction'. These points are elaborated in turn.

The reproduction of labour power, which purportedly provides the theoretical basis for urban politics, also involves private sector provision, domestic activities and biological reproduction. Mackenzie (1979) has argued that the neglect of these aspects of the reproduction of labour power follows from the analytical separation of 'production' and 'reproduction' in Castells' work:

> Shorn of its integral structural connection to production, reproduction becomes a theoretically isolated process, and only its most obvious surficial relations, those of consumption, remain. The complex relations and content of reproduction of labour become perceived as a process of individual and collective consumption, dominated by the latter. (Mackenzie, 1979, p. 19)

Production and reproduction are not discrete processes amenable to completely separate analysis, but are closely enmeshed

(McDowell, 1983; Mackenzie and Rose, 1983; Klausner, 1986). Consequently, production and reproduction are not, any more than production and consumption, male and female domains. Rather, gender differences are the product of the different ways in which production and reproduction combine within and affect the lives of women and men of all social and racial groups. The majority of both men and women are in waged work, as producers of goods and services. Both men and women participate (although not equally) in the domestic sphere, as husbands and wives, fathers and mothers, sons and daughters.

The reduction of the reproduction of labour power to collective consumption has also meant excluding aspects of daily life that are particularly important for women. As Wilson (1977b, p. 3) observes:

[f]or men, even when they are unemployed, work remains the core of their lives; certainly any political activity in which they engage is likely to be at their place of work. For women, on the contrary, even when they work, the home remains their sphere.

The significance for women of the domestic sphere is a manifestation of their central role in the reproduction of labour power: women continue to be the primary domestic workers and carers. As argued in the previous section, women are in the 'front line' over issues of consumption; women are also centrally involved in other aspects of the reproduction of labour power, including biological reproduction, the socialisation of children, cooking, cleaning and so on. Preteceille (1986, p. 147) has outlined:

Too often, collective consumption is equated with the public funding of social expenditures, without further discussion. But the very consumption processes and their social outcomes cannot be understood without taking into consideration who are the consumers and nonconsumers, what are their roles, their interests, their needs, and their contributions in processes of consumption, and what are the consequences on and for their lives.

Thus, the way in which people experience different forms of provision has received little attention. Moreover, objective

analyses of the economic significance of domestic work have little
bearing on subjective understandings of the role:

> a woman is always doing whatever she does for another reason,
> which she often takes to be the only reason: because she loves the
> people whom she looks after. The leftist leaflet may say that she
> services the workforce. As far as she is concerned she looks after
> her husband, 'Nan', and the kids. So women as domestic workers
> are caught in the pincers of a contradiction. We, the mothers and
> lovers who care, are at the exact point where all the good values of
> love and relationship are twisted, manipulated and threatened by
> the economic function of the family. (Cockburn, 1977b, p. 62)

Studies in urban politics have pointed to the material differences
resulting from reliance upon public or private forms of provision,
and have stressed the consequences for political alignment.
However, to focus solely on the economics of collective consumption ignores important aspects of human experience that relate
directly to the reproduction of labour power. These too may influence the basis and expression of political interests and it is to this
issue that attention now turns.

A feminist approach to urban politics

In the second section, attention was drawn to the significance of
gender in issues of consumption. Returning the term 'urban' to its
theoretical basis in the reproduction of labour power broadens the
scope of urban politics and allows a fuller understanding of the
importance of gender divisions. In the first part of this section we
consider how gender divisions influence the expression of political
interests. This leads us to argue for a feminist reformulation of the
term 'politics', as well as the term 'urban'.

Gender and the expression of political interests

Gender divisions influence interests in the reproduction of labour
power in two ways. First, as consumers, men and women enjoy
differential access to goods and services. It is necessary here to

differentiate between resources used collectively by households rather than, or as well as, individually. Differences in access between women and men as individuals often reflect differences in income. For this reason, women generally have greater difficulty than men in obtaining mortgages for home ownership (Austerberry and Watson, 1981) and have poorer access than men to many consumer goods and services. This may create important differences between households: one-parent families headed by women are usually poorer than those headed by men. However, within households access also differs. For example, the access of a household to a car may mean that a man has access while a woman relies on public transport (Tivers, 1985; also Pickup in this volume). Secondly, gender influences interests in the reproduction of labour power through the unequal division of domestic responsibilities between women and men. As primary carers, women tend to be more concerned than men with issues pertaining, for example, to children, the elderly and infirm. Further, to a much greater extent than men, women experience the home and the community as places of work: women in waged work are more likely than men to be employed in the immediate vicinity of their homes (Tivers, 1985) whilst women's unpaid domestic work necessarily occurs within the home. In addition, increasing numbers of women do waged work at home (Pahl, 1984). Consequently, women tend to be more concerned than men with their local residential environment, and therefore more likely

> to be provoked to campaign in their communities for better and more equitably located services, for better home and estate maintenance, for housing construction and neighbourhood design that meet their needs. (Mackenzie and Rose, 1983, p. 185)

Although gender divisions influence political interests, these interests have not always been taken up by political parties. State intervention in, and regulation of, the reproduction of labour power has tended to increase party political interest in the processes involved (see Dunleavy, 1986). However, this tendency is uneven and incomplete. It applies primarily where the state has assumed a major role in the provision of services (for example, housing, health and education). Partisanship is less marked at the local level of service delivery than at the level of national government where macroeconomic considerations are important. For example, in education, health and housing party politics have been more concerned with the determination of national policies and priorities, including levels of funding and the relationship between public and private provision, than with local decisions about implementation. Where local service delivery has provoked party conflict, it has generally been because of conflict with national government policies such as those relating to comprehensive secondary school reorganisation or council house sales. Other aspects of the reproduction of labour power remain almost wholly outside party politics, despite a significant degree of state regulation. This is particularly true of issues relating to biological reproduction such as abortion and reproduction technology (Stanworth, 1987).

Different reasons can be offered for the relative isolation of issues of 'reproduction' from mainstream political life. Several commentators have argued that the division of functions between central and local government is designed to reduce the tension between state activity concerned, respectively, with production and with 'reproduction' or consumption (Cockburn, 1977a; Friedland, *et al.*, 1977; Saunders, 1981). Thus, issues of production are the prerogative of central government, while state responsibility for the reproduction of labour power falls primarily to local government. The domination of party politics by the centre (parliament) tends to relegate the delivery of services to second place. Pursuing this approach, Saunders (1981) has argued that protests over consumption tend to be transitory, fragmented between themselves, issue-specific, locality-specific and no more than tenuously linked to more enduring political movements such as the Labour Party or the trade union movement.

This approach, however, ignores the relationship between gender and the reproduction of labour power: the extent to which the political isolation of issues of reproduction also involves the isolation of interests stemming from gender divisions is overlooked. An alternative explanation focuses on the limited political power of women. In Britain, women constitute 52 per cent of the electorate. However, the percentage occupying positions of political influence is inversely proportional to the power of these positions: women account for 40 to 50 per cent of local Labour and Conservative Party membership, about 15 per cent of local councillors and less than 5 per cent of MPs until the 1987 general election when the percentage rose to nearly 7 (Randall, 1982; Rogers, 1984). This pattern of under representation is often argued to underline the neglect of gender interests in party politics. However, caution is necessary because it is also possible to argue the converse: the neglect of gender interests in party politics can be cited as a cause of the under representation of women. There is probably some truth in both arguments but further insight can be gained by shifting attention away from the formal arena of party politics.

The under representation of women and of gender-based interests within the formal domain of party politics must not be confused with the absence of any political activity. First, women have made crucial interventions in the formal political arena despite their under representation, the movement for women's suffrage being the most notable example. Secondly, women participate in other forms of political activity, loosely termed 'informal', many of which focus on issues of reproduction, which have been a principal concern of urban politics. Evidence of the rates of participation of women and men in informal politics is difficult to obtain. However, reports of many campaigns and protests within this arena indicate the preponderence of women (Mayo, 1987; Women's Equality Group, 1977; but see also Edgell and Duke, 1983).

In her study of women and politics, Randall (1982) argues that the under representation of women in formal politics and their over representation in informal politics is the result of both constraints and choices. Certainly, women are inhibited from involvement in formal politics in a society in which 'women . . . remain tethered by their domestic responsibilities, and the attitudes associated with them, unable to compete on equal terms with men in the public political world' (Randall, 1982, p. 66). Thus, formal political equality is of little value to women in the absence of changes in gender relations (Stacey and Price, 1981). Informal politics tend to be more accessible to women: activities are local and there is greater flexibility in, for example, the timing of meetings, so that women can more easily combine participation with domestic and waged work.

It can also be argued that women actively prefer to participate in informal politics. Within mainstream politics, men and women participate as formally equal, autonomous individuals rather than as members of families or households. The same is not true within community politics: for example, women and men may participate much more explicitly as parents. Thus, in community politics there is a much greater degree of role continuity between 'political' and 'non political' activities. This is particularly important for women, for whom domestic and family roles have great salience. Moreover, the community and the home have different meanings for women than for the majority of men because, for women, regardless of their social class or ethnic origin, community and home are workplaces, whether or not there is also a workplace beyond the community. Consequently, for the housewife there is no separation in space, time or identity between 'work' and 'rest'. Thus, the home and the community as workplaces become the locus of political activity arising from issues of 'reproduction' in a manner parallel to that of the shopfloor in connection with production issues (Mackenzie and Rose, 1983).

A complex relationship exists between gender differences in political interests, and gender differences in political participation. The argument presented here is that community politics accommodates what is specific about both women's political interests and women's requirements for political organisation.

Challenging conventional definitions of politics

Saunders (1981, p. 276) has argued that '[T]hose whose primary concerns lie in furthering the conditions for the development of socialism will derive little return from either analysis of or activity in urban politics.' From a feminist perspective, McDowell (1983, p. 69) also remained sceptical of the radical potential of community-based political action:

> The continuing strength of the ideology of the home as haven rather than workplace, its significance as an object of conspicuous consumption and as a status indicator, the local provision of collective goods and services all reduce the prospect of gender-based urban social movements.

However, a basis exists for taking a more positive view of the potential of gender-based interests for promoting social change. These interests have a significance beyond their immediate goals in that they challenge conventional definitions of politics. Politics is popularly conceived of as a public activity, taking place within formal institutional settings, whilst the private, domestic, personal realm is considered to be apolitical. The two dichotomies, public versus private and political versus apolitical, are often mapped onto a third: male versus female (see Siltanen and Stanworth, 1984). These pairs of opposites are frequently used to make sense of the world, but feminists have challenged such ideas in several ways.

Historical evidence reveals that the distinction between 'public' and 'private' spheres is a malleable one, and Elshtain (1981) has argued that the dichotomy has served as an ideological device obscuring discrimination against women, rather than as an accurate description of social organisation. Further, the idea that politics occurs only in the public sphere, and that what is private is necessarily apolitical, has been forcefully challenged by the feminist insistence that the 'personal is political': feminists have demonstrated both that the supposedly private world of personal relations, domesticity, child care and so on, is inherently political in its definition of gender relations, and that the supposedly impersonal public arena is structured by particular forms of 'personal' interactions (such as those that silence women at trade union and other political meetings). With the recognition that politics is not an exclusively public activity but permeates all aspects of life, the attempt to superimpose these dichotomies onto gender divisions inevitably collapses. It may be true that women are under represented in the formal political domain, but it does not follow that women are apolitical, or that the lives of men are somehow public while those of women are private.

On the contrary, as argued above, women are well represented in a wide array of 'informal' political groups. In addition, women participate in large numbers in all-female organisations: in Britain, over 3 million women belong to such organisations as the Women's Institute, the Townswomen's Guild and the Mother's Union (Randall, 1982, p.46). Further, various feminist groups, such as Women's Aid, Rape Crisis Centres and the women's peace movement, are becoming increasingly well known and are attracting increasing levels of participation. The existence of these groups and associations testifies that gender is an important basis for social organisation. Although the Women's Institute and similar organisations are not self-consciously political and although feminist groups often eschew party politics, these groups and associations form an important vehicle by which women can articulate their interests over a wide range of issues. Further, their 'non-political' character itself reflects the narrow and male-biased way in which politics is conventionally defined.

The growth of urban protest and urban political activity provides rich but almost untapped evidence of the ways in which gender influences political consciousness and political organisation. Further, these new forms of political action implicitly challenge the common sense categories of public and private, political and apolitical. There is evidence that these challenges are being felt beyond the confines of community politics. For example, 'women's issues' (including sexual harassment, reproductive rights and child care provision, as well as equal pay and opportunities) are being taken up in the trade union movement; women's committees are springing up in local councils of all political persuasions (see Button, 1984; Goss, 1984) and there is some evidence of greater awareness of gender issues within the Labour Party. However, the development of political movements arising from, and committed to, changing existing gender divisions has not and will not be unproblematic.

Although gender may be an important influence on the political interests and activities of individuals, it interacts with other, equally important interests: women are divided by class and by race at the same time as sharing common experiences by virtue of their sex. The consequences of such divisions are sharply illustrated by Margaret Thatcher, who has successfully capitalised on commonalities in the experience of women without advancing the position of women in British society (see Campbell, 1987). From a different political perspective, black feminists have challenged the political practices of white women, pointed to the limits of unity based on gender, and established automomous organisations through which to develop and pursue their own politics (Amos and Parmar, 1984). Thus, our analysis indicates how gender interests and gender-based organisations have the potential to transform political practice, but it does not predict the emergence of a unified political movement based on gender.

Conclusion

In this chapter we have explored the role of gender in urban politics. We have demonstrated the failure of urban political studies to consider the significance of gender divisions in society, despite a reorientation of the field to focus on issues in which questions of gender loom large. This failure is not simply a function of disinterest at an empirical level on the part of academics, most of whom are men, but is also the result of inadequacies in the concepts employed. In particular, we have shown how the concept of 'collective consumption' is inappropriately and unnecessarily restrictive.

Recognising the limitations of existing approaches to urban politics is the first step towards reformulation. This we have pursued by exploring the significance of gender as a factor influencing political interests and political action. Our analysis suggests that informal or community politics is an important vehicle for the expression of interests arising from the particular roles of women in the context of contemporary gender relations. Moreover, we have argued that these political forms, together with women-only organisations, have a significance beyond the immediate issues raised. Through them, conventional, common sense distinctions between political and non-political, public and private, male and female, may be challenged. Although fragmented and sometimes in conflict, these groups have the potential to transform politics within and beyond the city.

Notes

1. This is not to deny that social relations in the workplace are also important in the reproduction of labour power. This is perhaps most clearly demonstrated in ethnographic studies of the transition from school to work (or training or unemployment) (see Willis, 1978; Troyna and Smith, 1983; Roberts, 1986).
2. Periodically, this position has been discussed within the Labour Party, for example after the defeat in the 1983 general election. However, the dominance of the parliamentary approach remains very firm.
3. The median time of return to work after the birth of a first child has fallen from 8.7 years for women bearing their first child between 1955 and 1959 to 3.4 years for women bearing their first child between 1975 and 1979. For women with two or more children, the proportion returning to work between the first and the latest birth has increased from 25 per cent to 47 per cent between these time periods, while the average number of years between the first and the latest births has declined from 6.2 to 5.3 years (Martin and Roberts, 1984, p. 128).

4. In London, for example, it has been estimated that women in full-time employment are sixty-six times more likely to have to care for a sick child than are men (Womens Equality Group, 1987).

Further reading

Antipode (1984) *Special issue on 'Women and the Built Environment'*, vol. 16(3).

McDowell, L. (1983) 'Towards an Understanding of the Gender Division of Urban Space', *Environment and Planning D., Society and Space*, vol. 1, pp. 59–72.

Mackenzie, S. and Rose, D. (1983) 'Industrial Change, the Domestic and Home Life', in Anderson, J., Duncan, S. and Hudson, R. (eds) *Redundant Spaces? Social Change and Industrial Decline in Cities and Regions* (London: Academic Press).

Martin, J. and Roberts, C. (1984) (eds) *Women and Employment: A Lifetime Perspective* (Department of Employment and Office of Population Censuses and Surveys) (London: HMSO).

Phillips, A. (1987) *Divided Loyalties: Dilemmas of Sex and Class* (London: Virago).

Randall, V. (1982) *Women and Politics* (London: Macmillan).

Siltanen, J. and Stanworth, M. (1984) (eds) *Women and the Public Sphere* (London: Hutchinson).

3

Balancing our space and time: the impact of women's organistion on the British city, 1920–1980

SUZANNE MACKENZIE

Introduction: women and the city

Three times in the last sixty years, women in Britain have been told to 'go home'. The first time was at the close of the 1914–18 War, throughout which women's public work had been both restricted and carefully presented as temporary (Beechey, 1977; Oakley, 1976; White, 1970). The second was at the close of the 1939–45 War, when women were told that their role in post-war reconstruction was to work full time in the homes, bearing and raising children and caring for their husbands, assisted by a range of new welfare state services and consumer goods (Douie, 1945; Myrdal and Klein, 1968; Riley, 1979; White, 1970). Thirdly, in the early 1980s in the context of a deepening recession and cutbacks of these same services, women were again being told to leave paid jobs to the men, their place was at home (Counter Information Services, CIS, 1976 and 1981; Labour Party, 1981).

The necessity for these renewed appeals indicates that the 'common sense' view that women's natural place was in the home has been a precarious one and that the maintenance of women's role as full-time domestic workers has required frequent social discipline. It also hints that women have not gone home and remained passive in the intervening periods. The monotonous repetition of these appeals also masks the fact that both the women and the homes to which they are urged to return changed significantly between 1918 and 1945 and between 1945 and the 1980s, in large part as a result of women's actions.

Throughout these seventy years, women's lives, their organisations and their self-perceptions have been conditioned by the fact that the primary job for most women, for most of their lives, has been the job of being a housewife and a mother.[1] Yet, over this period, the nature of this work, and the social environment in which it takes place, have altered radically. By extending control over their fertility and conditions of childbirth, women have broken the association between maternity and a life of full-time, often health destroying work, so that by the early 1960s, childbearing and nursing took up only 6 to 7 per cent of their adult lives (Myrdal and Klein, 1968). The control of women's lives by a biologically immutable cycle was, actually for some and potentially for all women, brought to a close.

The role of the housewife has also altered radically. The activities involved, the physical place occupied, the resources called upon have all changed with the advent of smaller families, new social services and consumer goods. Domestic work is still a demanding job but its content is changing. Much of the time that housewives in the 1920s and 1930s spent preparing food and cleaning the home is now spent travelling between shops and services in a more geographically extensive city. The social invisibility and geographic isolation of the housewife's job has been tempered and many of its activities politicised as the role spilled into the community. In addition, for more and more women, being a housewife has come to include the added dimension of financially contributing to family resources, taking on waged work or working for money at home. Between 1951 and 1971, the British labour force increased by 2.5 million; 2.2 million of these were women (CIS, 1976). By the 1960s, women's lives, organisations and images had become conditioned by a dual role; a primary job as housewife and mother was combined, for a majority of women for most of their adult life, with money-earning work.

This chapter documents these changes, demonstrating how women's organisation, by changing the conditions and content of their own lives, has led to different space–time patterns, perceptions and uses of urban resources by women and their families. The question of the relation between these changes in women's lives and the transformation of urban environments is not a wholly new one. But it is still relatively unexplored, and requires some theoretical and methodological introduction. Accordingly, some initial concepts are introduced to provide a framework for the subsequent empirical discussion of changes in women's organisation. These concepts are extended in the concluding section, which draws out some general themes characterising women's relationship to urban environments and suggests some of the implications for cities and our analysis of them.

Women and environments: some basic concepts

It has now been some twenty years since a popularly recognised women's movement re-emerged in Britain. The changes in women's lives which motivated this movement and the movement itself have become parameters of daily life. The introduction of feminist questions into geography, although impelled by these same changes and inspired by the wider feminist analysis and politics, has been more recent. (See Bowlby, *et al.*, 1982; Mackenzie, 1984; Monk and Hanson, 1982; Zelinsky *et al.*, 1982.)

Initial research on women and environments focused on 'proving' that women were a population subgroup which was sufficiently different to warrant specific geographic attention. This proof largely took the form of documenting how women as a group suffered specific spatial constraints. This led to an emphasis on the problems women encountered in contemporary environments, specifically the problems created by a division between the 'private' sphere of the home and the 'public' sites of production and power. Women's domestic roles in separate homes and residential neighbourhoods were seen to be the basis of restrictions on their access to and use of the wider resources of the city. (See Matrix, 1984; Stimpson *et al.*, 1981; Wekerle *et al.*, 1980; WGSG, 1984.)

This work was invaluable, both in dissecting the unidimensional model of 'man' in geographic models, and in focusing attention on the dichotomy of 'public' and 'private' spaces which had become an unexamined parameter of these models. (And of urban political analysis as a whole – see Chapter 2 in this volume by Bondi and Peake.) However, it tended to present women as 'environmental victims' – passively suffering restricted activity spaces or frantically scurrying between 'public' and 'private'. It is only recently that geographers have begun to examine the reverse side of the relation between women's activities and environmental change, to discuss women as environmental actors, contributing to building and restructuring the social environments in which they live.

A more reciprocal view of the relation between women and environments is now emerging, as research explores both the history of women's environmental relations and the organisational responses women are making to conflicts in their lives. This work is making it evident that the contemporary women's movement was not a decisive break with a tradition of passive, content and unorganised women.[2] Women, like men, have always organised and continue to organise to extend the resources available to assist in their work. But unlike men, the major work environment of most adult women in the home and community and their major responsibility is balancing the resources available or augmenting or stretching these resources to ensure that the family has an adequate or desired life-style.

Most women thus organise primarily from the home–community workplace. From this 'private' material base, women attempt to maximise family resources through adjusting the time and space they devote to various activities. For example, they readjust the time allocated to domestic work – the time required for giving birth, for care of children, and other adults, for maintaining the home. They also readjust the kinds of environments in which these go on, whether various activities take place in the 'private home', in other women's homes or in community spaces ranging from hospitals to neighbourhood playgrounds. They balance this work in the home and community with money-earning work. This money-earning work may take place in the 'public' productive sphere, in which case it alters women's own space–time patterns, or it may take place within the home and community, in which case it alters the nature of the domestic environment. Women's allocation of time and adjustment of space must thus constantly attempt to balance the amount of money, the number of goods and services and the amount of time required from the mother, the wife, the cook, the cleaner, and the wage earner, to achieve a desired family life-style.

The environments within which women work vary over time. The home and community both impose limits and offer opportunities as does the 'public' sector. Alterations in these social environments structure the necessary balance of space and time, and women readjust their use of space and time in response to these limits and opportunities. But this alteration in the social environment is not just a condition of women's action, it is also, in part, an outcome of their action. As women adjust their use of space and time, they create new environments and alter existing ones. They thus contribute to creating their own working environments.

In short, understanding the relationship between women and environments as one of reciprocal cause and effect requires some new concepts previously untried in geographical analysis. Given that one of the major and socially definitive responsibilities of women in contemporary society is domestic–community work, it is necessary to focus on how women organise to extend the resources available for this work. This requires extending the definition of organisational objectives from 'public' gains of political power or workplace control to include maximising necessary family re-sources, both in the form of goods and services and money. It also requires extending the definition of organisational arenas from 'public places' to include the home and community as working environments where goods and services are produced, some for direct use, some to be exchanged for money. We can see this organising taking place through a constant adjustment and reorganisation of spaces where women work and the time they devote to various activities.

The remainder of this chapter illustrates and extends the somewhat abstract framework presented above, looking at how women have adjusted their use of space and time in the past sixty years, and how this has contributed to altering space–time patterns in British cities as a whole. This discussion will focus on two fields which are fundamental in structuring the way women balance the space and time devoted to domestic work and waged work. It will trace changes in women's organisation from the interwar period, when most women devoted a large percentage of their time to domestic–community work, to the post-war period, when most women altered their working environments and time allocation to include money earning work. The concluding section will outline some of the implications of these organisational changes for the urban environment.

Women's organisation in the interwar and wartime period

Although in the pre-industrial and industrial periods most women had contributed to the family's material resources, either by working as part of a family productive unit or through waged work, by the early twentieth century, the majority of women were confining most of their energies to the newly created role of housewife. (See Clark, 1968; Ehrenreich and English, 1979; Mackenzie, 1987; Pinchbeck, 1969; Tilly and Scott, 1978.) Women's participation in the labour force, especially that of married women, generally declined after the 1914–18 War. During the 1920s and 1930s, women's domestic work was characterised by an identity of home and workplace. A women 'eats, sleeps, "rests" on the scene of her labour' (Spring Rice, 1981, p. 105). And while the association of 'home' and 'rest' rendered her work, and organisation around her working conditions, largely invisible to other family members, for domestic workers, 'work' swallowed up almost every moment. This was especially true of working-class women whose labour was materially difficult, described as going on in 'semi-barbarous conditions, intensified beyond calculation by the war and its consequences' (Brittain, 1979, pp. 575–6). Health and life itself were often precarious. Many families were living below the 'poverty line' and the mother's work and ability to cope often made the difference between health and malnourishment, or even between life and death (Spring Rice, 1981; Women's Group on Public Welfare, 1943). Yet, both working-class and middle-class women were being spurred on to greater efforts by 'home science' and rising standards of family care and of marital performance (Spring Rice, 1981; White, 1970).

Despite the hegemony of the housewife role in all aspects of women's lives, and despite the often crushing burden of work involved, women were neither passive nor silent in their homes and communities. Throughout the interwar period, housewives organised their conditions of work and life to compensate for the fact that their work was both dependent on and separated from the wage labour sphere. Many of these attempts were mediated through the internal distribution of family resources, and others through informal networks of family and neighbours or through the more formal women's organisations. Women's Institutes, Townswomen's Guilds, Women's Service Clubs and Women's Co-op Guilds not only provided information, education and social contacts for women, but also materially restructured working conditions through loaning equipment or providing new ways of shopping.

These, and a growing range of new women's groups, pressured for extensions of state services to make up the difference between male wages and the needs of the family.[3] Campaigns for improved public health and education and for family allowances – which recognised domestic work *as* work – were led by women's community groups (Branson and Heinemann, 1973; Spring Rice, 1981).[4]

The campaign for fertility control was also a significant part of women's attempts to control both their physical health and conditions of work. The birth control movement was always a movement by women, for women. Throughout the interwar period it not only established clinics but pressured for greater state responsibility for birth control (Leathard, 1980).[5] Women's greater control over their fertility became a vital social issue with the panic over declining birth rates in the 1930s and 1940s (Reddaway, 1939; Titmuss and Titmuss, 1942). Pressure, both coercive and positive, was exerted to inspire women to produce more children (Reddaway, 1939; Titmuss and Titmuss, 1942). This included the provision of better housing, long demanded by women's groups, for the socially desirable large family. Slum clearance and relocation policies had the unintended effect of increasing the isolation of many domestic workers through 'ending the extended family and community networks that previously helped informally to collectivise household work in urban areas' (Markusen, 1980, p. 31) and thus making housewives more dependent upon social resources for child care and emergency assistance (Harris, 1976).

Women's organisation in this period, while structured around extending resources for domestic work, was already opening up the 'private' home. The mass mobilisation of women during the 1939–45 War, and the radical changes this wrought in the 'private' household extended both the basis and the scope of women's activities. Women became part of the nation again, albeit 'with the assumption that both at home and in the labour force they were impausible' as 'real workers' (Riley, 1979, p. 106). The 'war effort', evacuation and shortages led to a range of new social machinery and social services, and women organised to help provide and consolidate control over these services.[6] These laid the basis for an optimism about the possibility of mass planning and the inception of a new relationship between the family and the state, to be brought to fruition in the post-war welfare state. But this new relationship also created new problems for women's lives.

Post-war welfare services took over and built upon many of the networks of services women had created in the preceding decades.[7] These networks had largely defined 'women's issues' as domestic issues, demanding resources to assist women's work, defending the 'private realm' of the home. Simultaneously, they opened up the 'private sphere' by demanding public resources for and recognition of the social and economic value of women's work in the home. This simultaneous defence and erosion of the 'private' and women's domestic role was incorporated into the welfare state.

Welfare services, like the women's networks which prefigured them, were designed to support a 'separate' family and to assist women in an assumed role as full-time mother and housewife,[8] yet, by the end of the war, this definition of women's activities was already outmoded, partly because of the implications of women's organisation. The 'opening up' of the private sphere of the family, begun in the interwar period, was extended by welfare services, ranging from means tests to housing inspection. The institution of welfare services multiplied the range of activities included in women's roles, while the expansion of state services and the consumer goods sector led to a rising demand for wage labour. Labour shortages, combined with rising expectations about domestic working conditions and with the continued need for work by the housewife-mother led to a new adjustment in women's space and time – the expansion and institutionalisation of dual roles for women.

Women thus entered the brave new post-war world supported by services which contradicted the reality of their lives. The welfare state at once specified and multiplied their activities and constituted a new force which had to be continually 'taken on' in an attempt to provide adequate resources for their lives. The next section discusses how women responded to these new conditions, creating a new urban space–time context through their organisation in the areas of fertility control, childbirth and child care.

Women's organisation in the post-war period

Extending control over fertility, childbirth and family patterns

The concern for a 'balanced' population and the debate around the means of achieving this has been present in British social planning since the inception of Malthusian theory.[9] Although an explicit policy had been resisted, discussions of population intensified as the fears of population decline in the 1940s and 1950s gave way to fears of global overpopulation in the late 1960s (Brooks, 1973; Leathard, 1980). In much of this excitement, women were seen primarily as units to which pressure was to be applied in order that they would produce the correct number of children. But for women, 'population figures' and 'demographic trends' were the basis of their conditions of work and health, their mobility and the resources available to them. Throughout the decades after the war, women made this evident with increasing force. Control over their fertility and conditions of birth became an increasingly social and political issue, fundamental to a new wave of women's networks, including a women's liberation movement, and to the material conditions of women's space and time.

Until the development of oral contraception, birth control was not considered as real medicine, and the Family Planning Association (FPA) continued to provide most professional advice while pressing, with other women's groups, for better facilities, and more state support for fertility control (Leathard, 1980).[10] In 1973, extra parliamentary pressure succeeded in making family planning part of the NHS. However, much counselling, research and education, and the campaigns against the medical dangers of 'contraceptive miracle' drugs and appliances continues to be carried out by the FPA groups and women's health networks.[11] Abortion services display a similar pattern of simultaneous pressure for 'public' facilities and provision of service. While the 1967 Abortion Act provided for NHS Services, constant threats to this Act and continued inadequacies of state services have resulted in the formation of a range of groups who, 'defend the Act' while also providing counselling and termination facilities.[12]

Childbirth services are also a combination of locally based self-help groups, nationally co-ordinated pressure groups and state services. In the post-war period, facilities for maternity and birth have become more of a social responsibility. In conjunction with improved health and housing conditions, this contributed to lowering rates of maternal and infant mortality, but it also led to what many felt was an excessive 'medicalisation' of birth. A growing range of groups have formed to press for 'humanised' hospital deliveries and to provide pre- and ante-natal care, education and mutual self-help.[13] These, like the fertility control and abortion groups, are a reflection of women's greater concern to control their lives, and at the same time extend their ability to do so.

These movements have also had direct and indirect impacts on family patterns and women's life-cycle. Relatively low and steady birth rates and compressed fertility has tended to decrease family size and has made it evident that maternity need not be a lifetime job. The growing number of women heading single-parent households have also shown that the male-headed nuclear family is not the only family form in which to bring up children. Combined with improved health services, control over fertility and birth have contributed to a longer life expectancy for women (Titmuss, 1968).

New family forms have lessened the biologically determined inevitability of women's lives, but also imposed new burdens, replacing a vulnerability to 'nature' with a vulnerability to 'society'. More decisions can be made, and must be made about family life. And more and more of these decisions have to be made with reference to, and in response to, a widening range of complex social factors outside the family's control. Growing numbers of women are faced with the contrast between the 'celebration' of motherhood and the paucity of services and support available to help women care for their children, while also carrying out other aspects of their dual roles. Of these latter services, child care is the most vital.

Extending control over child care

If the fact of becoming a mother is the most important single change in women's lives, the arrangements she is able to make in order to care for her children constitute the most consistent ongoing factor in constraining her space and time or in opening up new space and time.

Statutory child-care provision in Britain is both limited and fragmentary, reflecting an assumption that post-war women would be full-time mothers. Day nurseries are part of the Health Service, primarily intended to assist 'unfit mothers'. Nursery schools and classes are the responsibility of the Department of Education, and provide care primarily for children over 3 and usually on a part-time basis.[14] Waiting lists are often long and even this level of service is now under increasing pressure to cut back.

The inadequacy of statutory services has led to a growing range of networks which co-ordinate parent-run alternatives while also pressing for more 'public' responsibility.[15] The largest of the parent-run groups is the Preschool Playgroups' Association (PPA). Formed in 1961, by 1981 it had an estimated 13 500 affiliated playgroups servicing an estimated 270 000 children (*The Guardian*, 1981). Most of these are parent-run, or co-ordinated by a supervisor, often trained in a PPA course, and operate two to three hours a day, two to five days a week. There has also been a growth of 'mother and toddler' groups, informal meetings of mother and their 'under 3s' for a few hours a week. These too are generally parent initiated and run, often with the help of the PPA or Health visitors. In addition, there are a range of local self-help networks co-ordinating exchanges of child care and related services, sometimes sponsored by the Parent–Teachers' Association (PTA) or the National Childbirth Trust (NCT).

While many women use one or more of these networks at some time, they are inadequate for the needs of women with wage jobs. Most of these women rely on various forms of child minders, neighbours or relatives who work at home looking after other people's children, often as well as their own. In general, child-care services are a complex combination of statutory and collective parent-run facilities and informal individual arrangements. Most facilities are initiated and run by mothers themselves, for themselves and one another. And most women's child-care arrangements involve a complex juggling of space and time, fitting their various responsibilities around school hours, husband's or relative's hours, their need for monetary resources and for time with the children.

Child care is an especially important influence on the way women restructure their space and time. It has, from the perspective of its providers and users, three major functions: it is an element in women's waged work and it is an important source of employment for women.

First, child-care networks and facilities are a resource which structures the space–time patterns of women's domestic work. For many, collective networks are a substitute for extended family and community networks weakened by post-war slum clearance and suburbanisation policies, and by the growth of married women's labour force participation. These networks are a means of breaking down women's isolation and of establishing and maintaining local contacts for advice and exchange of services. Collective groups also provide some of the few safe and accessible public places for women with young children. Second, child-care services are a fundamental element in structuring the space and time of women's waged-work. The availability and quality of care, its location, its hours, its cost all determine, to a large extent, the kind of waged work women with children are able to do, the hours they can work, the distance and direction they can travel to wage jobs. Third, child-care services provide employment for a growing number of women, both as workers within the statutory sector and as playgroup supervisors or child minders.[16]

Fertility control/childbirth and child-care networks, set up to help women cope with the new conditions and constraints of their lives, are themselves changing the nature of both the domestic and wage-working environments, and dissolving the distinction between 'private' home and the 'public' workplace. Women are actively breaking down the complex division between public and private spaces through creating their own money-earning jobs which exist at the interface of home and wage work. In response to the fluid demands on their time, women are sharing jobs, co-ordinating wage working and child-care hours with other women. They are performing renumerative and socially necessary work for other women in their homes, caring for each others children, sewing each others curtains, teaching ante-natal classes and co-ordinating alternative consumer services. This, like the growing incidence of more traditional 'home work', is not new (CIS 1981; Crine, 1979). However, this adjustment of time and space to maximise resources is becoming an increasingly 'public' and political issue, largely through the efforts of the fertility, childbirth and child-care organisations. Not only are these 'interface' services increasingly organised on a local, regional and national scale, but they have growing ties to and actively intervene in their 'public', male-dominated equivalent – the trade union movement.[17] Most workers in statutory child-care sectors are union members and a growing number of parent-run and pressure groups have national and local trade union ties. (See Jackson and Jackson, 1979; National Campaign for Nursery Education, 1981; TUC 1980.)

All these groups are explicitly attempting to alter the relations between home and wage workplace in order that these relations more closely conform to women's changing lives. They are campaigning for recognition that wage workers are also parents and that parenting is socially and economically valuable work. Suggestions for facilitating this include altering wage-earning hours and conditions to reflect parenting responsibilities and providing community controlled alternative employment in the interface fields of child care, consumer services and health (NCC, 1981; PPA, 1980; Rowe, 1977). Meanwhile, such venues as self-training courses run by the PPA and NCT emphasise and extend the social importance and complexity of women's 'natural' parenting skills.

The lives of women with dual roles are complex, involving intricate arrangements in space and time, and severe constraints on space and time. In an attempt to cope with these constraints, women have created networks and places that cut across and actively alter the boundaries between 'home' and 'public places', which lie at the basis of the constraints. Some implications of this readjustment, both for urban environments and for urban analysis, are suggested in the concluding section of this chapter.

Conclusion: women changing cities

At the outset it was proposed that understanding how women's activities have contributed to altering British urban environments in the last seventy years requires that we focus on how women organise from the material base provided by the home–community workplace in order to maximise the resources available for their work. We can see this organising in terms of a constant adjustment of the space and time devoted to various activities. This adjustment is primarily a balancing of domestic work, which contributes to family resources through direct production of goods and services, with remunerative work, which contributes to family resources through earning money to buy goods and services produced by others.

The historical analysis above has indicated that women's adjustment of their time and space, in order to extend control over fertility/childbirth and extend resources available for child care, has resulted in increased interaction between the home–community and the 'public sphere'. This has had three interrelated effects on the urban environment; it has altered the nature of the home community, it has resulted in the creation of new spaces and networks in the city, and it has given rise to qualitatively different relations between 'private' and 'public' environments. The nature and some of the implications of these are examined below.

Extending control over fertility and improving maternal and child health has contributed to a general lowering of temporal compression of fertility and a concomitant increase in women's life expectancy. This has profoundly altered the most fundamental basis of domestic–community work; the size and form of the family. It has contributed to smaller families and to a generally ageing population, with attendant implications for demands on housing and services.

On an individual level, greater fertility control means that the number of children in the home comes under some control. At the same time, successful organisation to liberalise divorce laws and establish mothers' right to keep their children as independent parents means that the number of adults in a family is also amenable to more individual control. But both these forms of individually controlling the size and form of the family depend upon the use of external social resources, either birth control technology or family legislation. These are now largely provided by the statutory sector, but increasingly their maintenance depends upon their collective defence or the creation of alternative services by women themselves. Therefore, on the one hand, successful fertility control and improved childbirth conditions have allowed women to reallocate their time from bearing (and burying) an uncontrolled number of children. On the other hand, the maintenance of this control requires that they reallocate some of their time to more collective activities, largely the defence of existing facilities, and that they reorganise urban space to provide self-controlled venues for the provision of supplementary or alternative services for fertility control and childbirth when defence is insufficient. Fertility control groups and groups concerned with childbirth have thus directly created new physical spaces and new networks which, although isolated, are growing in size and importance, especially with threatened cutbacks in statutory provision.

In the field of child care, the informal networks and 'women's groups' which characterised the interwar period have been replaced by locally based collective organisations. These have some direct impact on urban time and space. The time that women devote to domestic work now often includes participation in playgroup work or sharing baby minding with neighbours. These groups have created new, local parent and child-orientated and controlled public spaces. These networks have also extended the socialisation of domestic-community work. Many of the activities of child care are performed in a qualitatively different way, emphasising the public recognition of parenting skills, the need for national co-ordination of child-care networks, and pressure within public forums for recognition of the social value of child-care work.

Perhaps most fundamentally, these new forms of fertility control, childbirth and child care create remunerative jobs at the 'interface' of 'private' home and 'public' arenas. Women are actively redesignating the home and community resources as 'working' resources, extending the 'living room' to include a playgroup, a workshop, a class room. They are dovetailing 'work time' and 'non-work time'. It is difficult to tell precisely when a women leaves off being at 'leisure' (for example, scrubbing floors, caring for her child) and begins work (for example, sewing a dress for a friend, caring for the neighbour's child). In general, women's adjustment of the use of space and time over the past seventy years has altered both the home–community sphere and the 'public sphere', largely through 'opening up' the home to a growing number of 'public' or collective influences. This has had the simultaneous and reciprocal effect of 'opening up' the public sphere to concerns of the home. Women's activities have shifted and permeated the boundaries of these spheres in two interrelated ways. On the one hand, the 'political' – those areas of life which are understood as amenable to principalled and rational action, is extended 'inward' from the vague and apparently inaccessible politics of the 'state', 'the economy' to the community, the home, the family and other aspects of interpersonal relations, including the sexual. On the other hand, simultaneously, those aspects of life which are 'personal' and 'private', the aspects over which our experience suggests we have some control, are extended outward. As biological reproduction, domestic work and family relations become more 'socialised', women's organisation, in response, extends the area over which we have control and choice; from the arena of sexuality to the organisation of family and household, to the neighbourhood, to the city and ultimately to national and international organisation.

Shifting and permeating the boundaries between 'private' and 'public' spaces and activities is perhaps one of the most fundamental changes being created in contemporary society. It is especially important to women, as their social definition and their activities stem from this contradictory separation. Both the production of goods and services and the reproduction and care of children and adults are necessary to the survival of any society. But unlike previous societies, contemporary industrial capitalism because of its emphasis on market criteria, has tended to separate these interrelated activities, first temporally and then, increasingly, spatially (see Mackenzie and Rose, 1983). It has never been possible fully to 'rationalise' the home or value the work women perform there. To the extent that this work has taken up most of women's time, and to the extent that their primary work space has been the domestic–community environment, they have been placed in a contradictory position; occupied with and defined in terms of the humanly essential work of biological and social reproduction in a society where power, planning priorities and even language derive from the 'public' sphere of producing goods and services. This separation has meant that women are either attempting to accommodate, or affect, the 'public' sphere from the socially subordinate 'private' sphere (as was the case with most interwar attempts to extend resources) or they are attempting to bridge the two, and meeting all the conflicts of time and travel constraints and contradictory messages documented in the extant literature on women and environments.

But this separation has much wider implications. It is reflected in the dichotomised form of contemporary cities. On the one hand, our cities contain industrial–commercial public areas – planned to rationalise production, devoid of reminders that nurture goes on in society. On the other hand, they contain residential areas – places where nurture, 'rest', emotional expression takes place, places apparently devoid of work. Most of our daily activities, our urban images are structured around this dichotomy, and it forms the basis of urban problems and planning priorities. For example, most urban transportation problems are problems of moving vast number of residents from 'home' to 'work' and back again. Discussion of urban services and resource allocation focus around balances between these two kinds of areas. Alteration of this separation will therefore restructure the basis of urban movement and planning.

Redesignating the home as a place for work, to produce both

consumable services and goods and money, is becoming increasingly important, not only to the future form of the city but to all people's daily lives. Cutbacks in statutory services mean that more needs must be met through informal networks. Rising unemployment among both women and men will cause more and more of the population to rely on redesignating the resources of the home and community to gain resources for survival. The forms of organisation long employed by women may become models for, rather than aberrations from, general political organisation.

In summary, the merging of public and private spaces and times is both the basis and the outcome of women's changing organisational priorities. While women ove the sixty-year period consistently organise to extend resources for their work, their organisation alters the environmental content and context of this work. The organisational priorities of interwar women – extending the resources available to workers in a separate and private sphere – have shifted to post-war concerns for solving problems located at the boundaries of domestic and public, the immediate and simultaneously social problems of childbirth and child care, in a society where the activities involved in being a housewife-mother are not only more socialised, but are only one aspect of women's lifetime activities.

The implications of these changes for women's (and men's) impact on future urban environments are not yet certain. But it is clear that seeing, and understanding these implications, as they are being created and experienced, will require some new kinds of geographical imagination, guided by an extension of the fluid concepts of 'organisation', 'resources' and 'time and space' suggested earlier in the chapter. These concepts soften, or even transcend, the analytic distinction between 'home and workplace', 'private and public', 'social and economic', which have underlain geographical research throughout the twentieth century. Such conceptual fluidity, disciplined by a sensitive eye and a hermeneutic empathy, will allow us to recognise and analytically incorporate the fundamental impacts which women and men have had and are having on our cities. They also open the possibility of understanding how the gender categories 'women' and 'men' are constituted and changed in relation to environmental change (see Mackenzie, 1983), and may thus allow us a new measure of control over the course of our lives.

Notes

1. I am not suggesting here, or elsewhere, that all women experience and create these changes in the same way. Their different class, racial and age positions provide different contexts and resources from which to act. However, on an abstract level, these relations do influence women as a gender defined social group and are, in fact, the primary constituents of that definition. Most of my discussion is concerned with family women – those who have children or other adults dependent on their domestic–community work – but the attribution of characteristics derived from this group is extended to all women.

2. The re-emergence of the women's movement was part of a radical, rooted continuity of feminist organising, the form of which was structured by women's working environments, and which broke from invisibility to 'public politics' in periods of massive social transition characterised by increasing socialisation of women's working conditions (see Mackenzie, 1980 and 1987).

3. For example, the National Association of Women's Clubs was formed in the 1930s to co-ordinate the activities of social service and mutual self-help networks. The Electoral Association of Women was founded in 1924 to inform women about electricity and provide a forum for expressing consumer's views. The National Association for Maternal and Child Wefare and the Charity Organising Society expanded and professionalised self-help and assistance to 'disadvantaged' families.

4. In addition to groups noted above these included a range of professional women's groups concerned with health and domestic working conditions, (Spring Rice, 1981; Women's Group of Public Welfare, 1943) as well as educational groups, such as the British Association for Early Childhood Education (BAECE), formed in 1923 to improve welfare of young children, and the Parent-Teacher Federation formed in the 1930s to co-ordinate home and school groups.

5. The first birth control clinic in Britain was opened in 1920 by Marie Stopes. By 1930, there were five national birth control societies which united into the National Birth Control Campaign. By 1938, the movement had sixty-one clinics (Leathard, 1980).

6. These groups included the London Women's Parliament – an association of housewives networks, Co-op Guilds and unions formed to propose a unified plan for mobilisation and to protect women wage workers, and the Women's Committee for Peace and Democracy formed to co-ordinate safe evacuation. (See Douie, 1945; Ferguson and Fitzgerald, 1954; Riley, 1979, on this period.)

7. In many cases the architects of the welfare state were identical to or informed by the groups noted above. In practical terms, for example, state responsibility for contraception eventually superceded some FPA work, home helps and social services took over the equipment loaning and case networks of the Co-op Guild, Women's Voluntary Service networks and the informal networks.

8. The Beveridge plan was predicated on full *male* employment, an adequate family wage and the specific definition of women as full-time housewives–mothers (see Wilson, 1977a).

9. Balance, in this case, was generally defined in terms of people relative to available resources, but often included 'desired' class or racial quotas.

10. FPA clinic expansion continued throughout the 1950s and 1960s – rising from sixty-five clinics in 1948 to a peak of 1016 in 1972 (Family Planning Information Service Fact Sheet 15).

11. Health protection groups include the Pill Victim's Action Group and the Campaign Against Depo Provera.

12. Abortion defence groups include the Abortion Law Reform Association, the National Abortion Campaign (formed in 1974), and the union affiliated Labour Abortion Rights Campaign (formed in 1976), the Co-ordinating Committee in defence of the 1967 Abortion Act which had fifty-five member affiliates in 1981 (formed in 1976), the British Pregnancy Advisory Service and the Pregnancy Advisory Service, as well as local women's termination services.

13. The largest of these is the National Childbirth Trust, formed in 1956 to improve women's knowledge about childbirth. It sponsors ante-natal and breast-feeding classes by NCT trained teachers, as well as co-ordinating post-natal support groups and pressing for 'humanised' hospital delivery. The Association of Radical Midwives was formed in 1976 to encourage women's active participation in birthing, the Maternity Alliance formed in 1980 to press for improved medical, financial and social support for parents and children. The Society to Support Home Confinements, the Lalèche League and the Association for the Improvements in the Maternity Services all pressure for improved public services while providing practical mutual aid.

14. In 1980, it was estimated that 14 390 of children aged 3 to 4 in the United Kingdom were attending some form of nursery education (National Campaign for Nursery Education Fact Sheet).

15. Pressure groups include the BAECE (see note 4), the National Campaign for Nursery Education, established in the mid 1960s, which presses for more free state nursery education, and the more militant National Childcare Campaign, set up in 1981, as well as a range of local defence groups and union affiliated groups.

16. Wages within the non-statutory sector are almost universally low and often erratic. (See National Childminders' Association, 1969, and Pre-school Playgroup Association.)

17. For example, local playgroups are generally affiliated to a PPA city-wide co-ordinating group which contributes to regional and, in turn, national co-ordinating levels, all of which provide various services to more or less autonomously run individual playgroups. A similiar 'bottom up' federated structure is evident in the National Childbirth Trust, as well as in pressure groups such as the National Campaign for Nursery Education, the National Abortion Campaign, and the Family Planning Association.

Further reading

Mackenzie, S. (1986) 'Women's Responses to Economic Restructuring: Changing Gender Changing Space, in Barrett, M. and Hamilton, R. (eds) *The Politics of Diversity: Feminism, Marxism and Canadian Society* (London: Verso).

Mackenzie, S. and Rose, D., (1983) 'Industrial Change, the Domestic Economy and Home Life, in Anderson, J., Duncan, S., and Hudson, R. (eds) *Redundant Spaces? Social change and Industrial Decline in Cities and Regions* (London: Academic Press).

Matrix (1984) *Making Space: Women and the Man-made Environment* (London: Pluto).

Women and Geography Study Group of the Institute of British Geographers (1984) *Geography and Gender: An Introduction to Feminist Geography*, especially the chapter on urban spatial structure (London: Hutchinson and Explorations in Feminism Collective).

4

From corner shop to hypermarket: women and food retailing

SOPHIE BOWLBY[1]

Introduction

Two hundred years ago in Britain, as in Western Europe and North America, the retailing of food and other goods from fixed shops was an insignificant economic activity. The subsequent development of capitalism in these countries has involved the commodification of the process of exchange in the form of the development of a complex wholesale distribution and retailing sector of their economies. This development of retailing in capitalist countries has been part of the creation of a wider set of social and economic relations through which home-based consumption simultaneously stimulates and depends on the production of goods and services by waged workers. Feminists have long argued that the ways in which activities in the spheres of 'work' and 'home' relate to and interact with one another are of central practical and theoretical concern to women. Nowhere is this more true than in the area of food shopping. This chapter will examine how development and change in the system of retailing and home-based consumption in Britain has been linked with changes in the waged and unwaged work of women.

Shopping for and preparing food is largely the province of women throughout the advanced capitalist countries of the world today (Scott, 1976; Bowlby, 1984). In Britain at present some 79 per cent of households are made up of married couples with or without children and in almost all such households food shopping is the woman's responsibility (Bowlby, 1984; Gershuny, 1982; Pickup, 1983). Meal preparation as in other societies is also usually the women's task, so that provisioning the family is a major part of married women's everyday activities.

Women's role in providing the family's meals is underpinned by current conceptions of women as 'nurturers'. An important element in our present-day conception of womanhood and of female sexuality is the idea that women should love, nurture and tend their men and their children (Foord *et al.*, 1986). Providing food plays a prominent part in this conception for both women and men. For example, shopping for food and preparing meals are seen by the majority of women as the most important of housewifely tasks (IPC, 1970). This is not surprising given the central role meals are felt to and do have in expressing women's love for family members, preserving family equanimity, and in affecting family health (Murcott, 1983; Luxton, 1980; Coward, 1984). Food shopping is an integral part of the process of both literally and psychologically nourishing and reproducing labour.

Nurturing the family within the home is an important element of women's role, but women also contribute to the well-being of family members through their waged work. About 60 per cent of married women in Britain today work for wages and for the majority this work is seen primarily as a way to share in paying for household 'necessities', including food, although independence and enjoyment of work are also important reasons for women taking paid employment (Martin and Roberts, 1984). The wages women earn help to fuel households' consumption of and demand for food and retail services. Moreover, many women not only spend their wages on such services but earn them in retail employment. In Britain, the entire wholesale distribution and retailing sector of the economy employs some 3 million people (OPCS, 1981). The retail labour force accounts for just over 2 million, and a high, and increasing, proportion of this retail labour force is made up of women. By 1984, women represented 65 per cent of the workforce in food retailing (Reynolds, 1983; Sparks, 1984).

While both working- and middle-class women are expected to feed their families directly and through their earnings, experience of the world of food provision and food retailing for each is very different. It is working-class women who have made up the new female retail workforce and who suffer the low pay and poor employment opportunities characteristic of retail work. Although middle-class women also suffer from inequality in employment relative to men, their own and their husbands' position in the labour market leads to higher and more secure household incomes than those of working-class families. Thus, the resources that women of different classes are able to use to carry out the tasks of food shopping and meal preparation – car transport, child care, household machines and food products – differ strikingly. These differences in resources are reflected in variations in the type of food retailing available in residential areas of different class composition. Such class differences in resources and retail employment have also been apparent in the past.

We therefore find that today women play a dual role in relation to food provision. First, in the world of food retailing they are not only the principal consumers but also the principal producers of retailing services. However, the latter role is principally played by working-class women. Secondly, in the world of the family, both middle- and working class women provide 'nurture' in the form of planning, shopping for and preparing meals. In addition, they also provide 'nurture' through their wages which help to pay for the food to make the meals.

The development of this current version of women's 'proper' role within the family has been closely linked with the expansion of capitalism and the extension of commodity relations into new areas of social life. During the nineteenth and twentieth centuries this expansion has involved the development and implementation of technical and organisational changes in production which have facilitated the growth of profitable mass production of goods. This growth in mass production has gone hand in hand with the expansion of home-centred mass consumption. New material aspirations for home life have been developed, with a concomitant increase in emphasis on home-centred sources of identity and satisfaction. In this century home-based consumerism has been linked to the rise of home ownership and the expansion of suburbia. The extension of consumption within and related to the home during the nineteenth century involved the decline of home-based production, the spatial separation of 'home' and 'work' and the demarcation of the home and the domestic sphere as women's 'place' (WGSG, 1984; Davidoff *et al.* 1976; Mackenzie and Rose, 1983).

The development of capitalism has involved a seeming paradox for women – an increased emphasis on the home and on women's importance within it in caring for the family, alongside an increasing dependence for the specification and performance of these tasks on goods and services produced outside the home. Moreover, many of these goods and services are now themselves produced by women in newly established relations of waged work. Such changes in the definition and execution of domestic labour have been accompanied by major changes in the scale and nature of the marketing and retailing system. For example, many parts of food production and preparation have ceased to be unwaged 'private' labour performed within the household. Most bread, for instance, is now manufactured, most vegetables are grown commercially and many meals come from the freezer or a tin. These foods are selected and purchased by the 'housewife' in a retail shop, the timing of the purchase, the distance travelled, the choice and price of goods are constrained by the shops available to her and her selection of goods is influenced by marketing and media information. The creation and marketing of new food products do not simply meet an existing demand but redefine and enlarge the possible ways in which meals can be presented and provided and increase the demand for the services of the retailer.

The effective development and satisfaction of the mass urban market for commercially produced, manufactured and processed foods which exists today has been, in part, dependent upon the creation and periodic restructuring of the food retailing sector. This restructuring has not occurred evenly over time or space and has involved changes in the nature of retail employment and in shopping behaviour, which have been of considerable but differing significance to both working- and middle-class women.

In the next section, some of the ways in which food distribution has linked the spheres of production and reproduction for women of different classes are illustrated by examining the relationships between changes in women's domestic and wage-earning roles and changes in retail organisation during two specific periods. First, the nineteenth century, which saw increasing pressure for women to retreat into domesticity; and secondly, the post-Second World War period of this century, which has seen strikingly rapid increases in the involvement of women, particularly married women, in waged work. Both periods were ones in which food retailing in Britain changed significantly. The main focus here concerns changes in the people involved in different parts of the process of transferring food from producer to middle-class and working-class consumer, whether this work was paid or unpaid and on how changes in the nature of the work involved were related to changes in the spatial organisation of retailing. After this look into the past, the final section of the chapter considers some of the future implications of current technical and organisational changes in food retailing, in relation to potential changes in women's social roles.

Past changes in food retailing and women's domestic role

Retailing and the separation of 'home' and 'work' in the nineteenth century

With the mass movement of population into the towns and cities during the first half of the nineteenth century, the opportunities for home production of food became limited and hence the demand for the retailing of food increased. The earlier, relatively important position held by women in the management of the household economy was still maintained in relation to family expenditure, and women thus had the responsibility for household shopping (Scott and Tilly, 1975). However, the poor living conditions and long hours of factory or sweatshop employment which were common for women of the working class gave little time for shopping or cooking, while low incomes, and cramped and inadequate housing kept down the quantity and quality of food products demanded. Time-saving shopping, small quantities of goods, and some pre-cooked foods were provided by local street markets, itinerant traders, and very small, local shops which remained open some sixteen hours a day.

Street trading was a way in which the poorest could eke out a living since entry to the trade required little equipment or formalities. Both married and single women worked as street sellers of food: in London women traders specialised in the sale of certain types of food: 'fish (principally shrimp, sprats and oysters), fruit, vegetables (mainly sold by widows) . . . tea, coffee, rice-milk, curds and whey' (Alexander, 1976, p. 101). The stock sold in the markets and by itinerants was often bought from fixed shops so that at this period the two methods of selling complemented rather than conflicted with one another. Women often kept the tiny general shops selling food and household necessities that were common within the spatially segregated working-class disticts that were now developing in urban areas. Many of these shops simply comprised a room within a house, and keeping such a shop was a common way for a widow to survive or for the wife of a workman to add to the family income. Although these shopkeepers and street traders drawn from and selling to the working class can be classified as members of the petty-bourgeoisie, during the early part of the nineteenth century neither their incomes, way of life nor their aspirations marked them off from the members of the working class amongst whom they lived. Whatever the conflicts between buyers and sellers, the retail system in working-class areas was predominantly a system arranged for their mutual survival; for 'getting-by' rather than for profit and the stimulation of consumption. As such it provided a strong contrast with the system of retailing developing in the new, spatially separate, middle-class residential areas.

Amongst the growing middle classes a new urban life-style was developing, involving a new attitude to the home and to women. The home began to be seen as a 'haven' for men from the brutalising influence of work; a haven ordered and managed by women, idealised figures untainted by the world outside (Davidoff *et al.*, 1976). Moreover, it was thought 'ungenteel' for women to engage physically in housework and, in particular, in cooking. The new middle-class life-style required a substantial use of servants, an increasing emphasis on the house and its furnishing, and an elaboration of household tasks and standards of house presentation. This new ideal was linked to the spatial as well as the social separation of 'home' and 'work' and the development of specialised residential districts away from the town centres with their mixture of housing, markets, craft workshops and new retail establishments.

The increasing consumption of the new urban middle classes (and skilled artisans) encouraged the growth of fixed food shops in town centres and in the new middle-class areas. There were, for example, shops selling relatively expensive imported goods – tea or dried fruits – as well as more mundane articles. Apart from the owner (usually male), the labour in such shops generally was supplied by family members as well as by male apprentices. In particular, wives and daughters continued the traditional role of the skilled tradesman's wife, helping to keep the books as well as working in the shop (Hall, 1982; Davis, 1966). Such food retailing was a skilled occupation since a considerable amount of food processing – selecting, cleaning, sorting, and cooking – was carried out by the retailer and his assistants; moreover, their middle-class customers expected high standards of service and advice. Initially, these shops remained in the town centres but by the mid-nineteenth century, suburban food shops were beginning to appear in most large towns and a clear physical identification of convenience retailing with the sphere of the home and domestic labour began to emerge (WGSG, 1984).

By the latter half of the century incomes had started to rise, middle-class women went to the food markets and provision shops less frequently themselves, and instead relied on the labour of servants (usually female) and retailers' delivery workers (usually young men) to carry out the physical task of household shopping. Orders were collected from the house by the fixed-shop retailers themselves or by their assistants. Although middle-class women did go to the shops to examine and choose food and groceries, and to maintain the important personal relationships with the retailer on which good service might depend, their involvement in shopping was as the 'household manager', not as a 'household worker'.

The idea that a respectable woman's proper place was in the home also began to influence the involvement of married women in the retail shops serving the middle classes. Successful and prosperous retailers and their families were themselves members of the new middle class and aspired to an appropriately middle-class life-style and suburban living. Lock-up shops, whose proprieters lived elsewhere, were becoming more common by the mid-century (Alexander, 1970). This separation of home and shop, and the new ideas about women's central role in the separate sphere of the home, tended to decrease the part played by the wives of successful retailers in the family business. Furthermore, the growth of increased formality and complexity in bookkeeping and business methods required a training and education to which few women had access (Hall, 1982).

Soon after the mid-century, married working-class women's participation in formal waged labour and factory employment appears to have declined across much of the country, although it remained relatively high in the textile areas of the north-west. The reasons for these changes are complex and disputed (Brenner and

Ramas, 1984) but male trade-unionists' pressures for a 'family wage', legislation against long hours of work for women, rising real incomes and the adoption of the new ideals concerning women's domestic role all played a part. Amongst the better-off working-class families the involvement of married women in paid work declined and while it remained central to the survival of the poorer families (although often based at home), their hours of work outside the home were reduced as the length of the average working day was cut. With more flexible time-schedules, higher real incomes and increased consumption, their dependence on the 'delivery service' of the itinerants declined and their own use of fixed shops increased. The relationship between women's hours of work outside the home and the time available for food shopping and cooking is emphasised by the differences between the cooking and consumption patterns in the textile areas and those in other parts of the country. For example, consumption of the 'convenience' foods of bacon and cheese was higher in the textile areas (Alexander, 1970). There was also what Roberts (1982) terms a 'textile diet' – hotpots (prepared at home but cooked in bakehouses while the adults were at work and the children at school), ready-cooked tripe and pies, and fish and chips.

The last quarter of the nineteenth century also saw the rapid expansion of the multiples.[2] Rising real incomes amongst the working classes; increases in population; new, cheap, mass-produced or imported foods from Britain's colonies; the development of limited liability companies; together these developments provided the opportunity for some retailers to realise economies of scale (Jeffreys, 1954). By the 1890s food multiples such as the International Tea Company, Lipton Ltd and the Home and Colonial Tea Company had about 200 outlets each. The development of the multiples marked the beginning of the organisation of retailing to make large-scale profits and the transformation of fixed shops from units that existed solely to fulfil customers' wants to units designed and planned to attract customers and create wants (Ibid., p. 37). It was a transformation that depended on the existence of a substantial working-class market. However, despite their significance as an innovation in retailing, the multiples as a whole only accounted for about 10 per cent of the food trade by 1900 (see Table 4.1 below).

Another significant development during the second half of the

Table 4.1 *Percentage of total retail sales of groceries and provisions taken by different type of retailer*

	Co-operative societies	Multiple retailers	Other retailers
1900	14–15	4–7	77–82
1910	16–18	9–12	70–75
1920	18–21	13–16	63–69
1930	19–21	18–20	59–63
1939	22–24	22–25	51–56
1950	21–23	23–25	52–56
1961	21	27	53
1971	15	44	42
1981	14	63	24

Source: The figures from 1900 to 1950 are taken from Table 31, Jeffreys, 1954, p. 163. The figures for other retailers for this period include sales from department stores and by producer/retailers as well as independent retailers. The figures for 1961–81 are taken from Department of Industry statistics presented in IGD (1980) *Developments in the Grocery Trade*, IGD presentation at Reading University.

nineteenth century was the Co-operative food shop; operating on non-profit principles, these shops also had begun to supply the industrial working-class market in the North and in Scotland. Despite the very different philosophies of the co-operatives and the multiples, both, as relatively large-scale purchasers, offered considerable advantages as outlets for the products of the new large-scale food manufacturers – indeed, the Co-operative Societies produced some of their own products on a large scale. Both, therefore, aided the expansion of a mass market for manufactured foods. The reduction in the real price of food certainly led to an improvement in the working-class diet but the new large-scale retailers and manufacturers, as well as middle-class philanthropists, also encouraged working-class women to aspire to 'high' food standards which required more domestic labour for their fulfilment. Thus, they were part of the gradual transformation of retailing amongst the working class from a system of survival to a system based on profit.

Shopkeeping remained an important method of survival for many wives and widows drawn from the working class. However, as members of the petty-bourgeousie, shopkeeping families began to be seen and saw themselves as socially superior: 'shopkeeping was the most usual way of achieving upward social mobility for the

aspiring members of the working-class . . . As a group, shopkeeping wives were moving in the 1890s towards the family consumer
economy in which items hitherto regarded as luxuries by the
working-class became necessities' (Roberts, 1982, p. 149). But the
advent of the multiples and the co-ops was creating a new group
within food retailing employment – the paid shop assistant. At this
period they accounted for only a tiny fraction of food retail
employees and the majority were men, although in other branches
of retailing, young single women shop assistants were no longer
unusual (Jeffreys, 1954).

Thus the changes in the behaviour expected of women that took
place in the nineteenth century produced different effects on
working- and middle-class women's shopping behaviour. Amongst
middle-class women, the view that a woman's sphere should lie only
within the home produced a *withdrawal* from active involvement in
the physical task of shopping. Amongst working-class women the
reverse was true. Their active involvement in travelling to and from
the shops and its significance as part of their domestic labour grew.
The lack of transport or storage facilities available to working-class
women meant that shops had to be very close to their homes. This
was reflected in the early popularity of itinerant traders and, later,
in the location strategies of the first multiples (Ibid.). This factor
was less significant for shops selling to the middle-class market,
although the need to keep up a personal relationship and the costs to
the shopkeeper of providing an ordering and delivery service also
limited the extent of their catchment areas. For married women of
both classes who were retail workers, shopkeeping provided a route
to upward social mobility and, for the successful, the eventual
withdrawal from active involvement in retail work. However, for
many working-class women such success was never achieved and
shopkeeping remained a precarious means of survival.

*Retailing in the post-war period: the development of woman's dual
role*

From 1900 until the Second World War the nature of the work
involved in household shopping did not change fundamentally. The
multiples and co-operatives continued to grow and by 1939
accounted for about 46 per cent of food retail sales (Jeffreys, 1954).

They had also improved the quality and range of goods provided and many now offered delivery services. As a result, the contrasts between the retail services provided to middle- and working-class women were less extreme than before. By this time a dense network of fixed shops had been established in suburban areas and distances to local shops were small.

For both middle- and working-class women, shopping was frequent (daily or several times a week) and local, generally involving personal loyalty to particular shops. The frequency of shopping amongst the middle classes (who now formed a significant proportion of the population) increased during this period as a result of the trends towards smaller houses and households, and a greater reliance on an increased variety of manufactured and packaged food.

There were two notable changes in the nature of food retailing in Britain during this period. The first was the dramatic reduction in shop hours (Alexander, 1970). The second was the increasing employment of female shop assistants in food shops after the First World War. This re-entry of women into food retailing employment paralleled other changes in women's employment during the inter-war years. During this period female employment grew in some expanding manufacturing industries such as light engineering and electrical goods and also in clerical work, and middle-class women gained entry to some of the professions. Although many contemporaries considered these developments to signal growing female emancipation, these new employment opportunities were largely confined to single women. The percentage of married women in formal waged employment remained at about 10 per cent throughout the inter-war years. The picture was the same in retail work where it was only in family run shops that married women played any significant role as retail workers. These new employment opportunities offered single women alternatives to working as domestic servants, and the proportion of employed women in this sector declined from 42 per cent to 32 per cent, between 1901 and 1931, however, the number of domestic servants per head of population actually increased slightly. Thus for a middle-class women much of the irksome labour of food shopping and food provision was still carried out by paid workers.

The inter-war pattern of food retailing and food shopping was not to endure long. Soon married women were to make up a large proportion of retail workers, self-service was to become the norm, delivery services and servants a thing of the past, and increasing numbers of married women were to enter paid work. Immediately after the Second World War such changes seemed unlikely, but in the late 1940s and early 1950s women were encouranged to return to the home from their wartime employment in order to ensure population growth and to create a happy family and community environment (Wilson, 1980). It was felt that women should concentrate on 'the more stimulating and rewarding aspects of housework, child care and beautification of the home' (Ibid., p. 22). To this end the drudgery of their work in the home should be removed through the use of modern household appliances in well-planned living conditions. The newly important planning profession reflected these ideals in their designs for food retailing. The removal of drudgery was to be achieved by siting food shops within convenient walking distance of housewives, with particular attention to the needs both of the elderly and of mothers with young children. Ideally the shops were to be sited so that, if desired, shopping trips could be combined with other daily domestic journeys, such as taking the children to school. Thus the typical pattern of shop location advocated at this time was that of a shopping centre with some forty or so shops in the middle neighbourhood units of about 10 000 people, with, in addition, one or two subcentres containing about twenty shops. Shops for everyday needs should be within a quarter of a mile of every home. There would also be a major town centre for weekly shopping (Keeble, 1952).

Planning prescriptions for food shopping in the early 1950s re-emphasised the existing separation of areas of domestic labour from those devoted to production based on waged labour (McDowell, 1982; Mackenzie, 1980). They also played down any differences in access between women arising from different class or income positions. However, the majority of people lived in existing towns with a well-defined pattern of spatial segregation by class, a pattern that the separate development of new council and private estates did nothing to alter. Hence, despite the ideals of the planners, the small neighbourhood shopping centres that were developed in the new housing areas, or that were maintained in older areas, remained class specific and differentiated in quality in relation to the income of their customers. Furthermore, both planned and unplanned neighbourhood shopping centres soon began to change. By the end of the 1950s, the self-service supermarket was beginning to make inroads into the market share of traditional grocers.[3] The number of grocery and food outlets declined, partly as a result of this competition and partly because of inner area redevelopment policies, and there was increased spatial concentration of retailing. Planned neighbourhood centres and subcentres of the 1950s and early 1960s usually could sustain only eight to twelve shops. More recently, the development of superstores and the closure of smaller high street and neighbourhood supermarkets has intensified the trend towards spatial concentration of retailing.[4] This spatial concentration has been paralleled by increased concentration of ownership, so that the distribution of food products has become controlled by fewer firms. Furthermore, these firms have become increasingly powerful in relation to manufacturers so that they now exert considerable power over the production as well as the distribution of food (McGoldrick, 1984; Lewis, 1985).

This major restructuring of the organisation and location of food retailing sprang from pressures to increase turnover and profits in a trade at a time when the proportion of consumers' incomes spent on food was declining. It involved important changes in the nature of the retail services offered to customers and in the employment of women. First, more and more grocery shops, both supermarkets and smaller shops, became self-service shops. The role of the shop assistant in advising, fetching goods and advertising new products was reduced dramatically. Delivery services also were first reduced and then largely abandoned by the multiples and the co-operatives. Secondly, the new supermarkets began to employ both more married women and also more part-time workers. The proportion of the food retailing labour force accounted for by part-time women workers increased from 10 per cent in 1951 to 38 per cent in 1981 (OPCS, 1951, 1981).

The moves amongst retailers to self-service, a predominantly female labour force, and to part-time workers were prompted in part by a desire to cut costs. In the early 1960s, McClelland (1963) estimated that wages represented the largest single item of costs in grocery retailing and that a shift from counter-service to a self-service supermarket operation of similar size could cut a third off the wages bill. But the need to cut labour costs was itself linked to the growing difficulty of finding cheap labour in an expanding economy. Employing women, who could be paid lower wages than men, was one solution. However, the expansion of demand for labour was offering women other work opportunities. Retailers, who traditionally offered very low wages, found themselves competing with other female-employing industries paying higher wages. The use of part-time workers was one response to this (Ibid.), a response which relied heavily on the employment of married women who were often only able to work part-time hours. This use of part-time workers was also further encouraged by the overall growth of employment amongst married women. Working women shopped only during lunch hours or evenings and thus produced greater temporal 'peaking' in demand at supermarkets and a need for more temporary labour on check-outs and for shelf-filling (Lewis, 1985).

As a result of these pressures the proportion of women employed in food retailing has increased throughout the post-war period. Women now form the majority of the 'un' or 'semi'-skilled food retail workforce but retail management remains male dominated. Retailing employment is no longer a significant means of independent survival or of social mobility for working-class women. Much retail work has become deskilled and repetitive (Auld Committee, 1984; Lewis, 1985). Moreover, female retail workers have become some of the worst paid workers in the country (see Table 4.2).

Table 4.2 *Low pay in major female-employing jobs: 1983*

Ten worst paid jobs	£ per week (gross)
Hairdressers (female)	60.5
Waitresses (female)	72.5
Shop assistants (female)	73.4
Check-out operators (female)	74.9
Kitchen hands (female)	75.7
Barmaids (female)	77.2
Sewing machinists (female)	77.6
Receptionists (female)	80.1
Counter hands (catering) (female)	80.3
Cleaners (female)	81.8

Source: CES (1985). Table prepared from the *New Earnings Survey*, 1983; and taken from *Labour Research*, vol. 72, no. 11, November 1983.

The move to supermarket trading depended for its success not merely on cutting labour costs but on expanding the rate of turnover generated per square foot, so that economies of scale in purchasing, stocking and advertising, as well as in employment, could be realised. Large sites and buildings were needed, requiring considerable capital investment and this gave an advantage to the larger multiples. In order to achieve high turnover, supermarkets also needed a reasonably large and affluent population of consumers within their catchment areas who could take advantage of the benefits of the 'one-stop' shopping offered by this new type of food shop. It is not surprising that the early supermarkets in Britain grew fastest in London and the surrounding Home Counties. Their growth was encouraged by the general increase in household incomes – an increase which owed much to the wages brought home by married women. The rise in car ownership associated with these higher incomes also encouraged supermarket use by allowing households to purchase in bulk. But although household car ownership doubled between 1955 and 1965 (Ministry of Transport, 1965) it was far from universal and by 1971 48 per cent of households still had no car (Central Statistical Office, 1972). Moreover, very few women had daytime access to a car (Hillman *et al.*, 1973). In households without a car the increased spatial concentration of food shops and, in particular, of supermarkets, meant that for many women going shopping required longer and more tiring journeys on foot.

While retailing and shopping were undergoing these changes, so too were the conceptions and actuality of women's domestic role. There was increasing acceptance of 'working wives', but this acceptance was conditional on women performing the 'dual role' of worker and housewife. Indeed, for most women, going out to work was seen as a way of contributing to the welfare of their families by providing a better income. Thus the growth in married women's employment did not fundamentally challenge the view that a wife's primary duty is to care for her family – it merely redefined the nature of 'care'. Women were expected to stay at home when their children were young; part-time employment could be taken once they were at school. Only when they had raised their families should women return to full-time employment (Myrdal and Klein, 1956; Wilson, 1980). Moreover, there was a continued and growing emphasis in the media on consumption as the key to an improved quality of home life. In particular, advertisers and the increasingly popular women's magazines urged the housewife to spend some of the enlarged family income on new and more exotic foods, cleaning products, and household equipment. The media began to take over the role of adviser to the housewife on cooking and marketing, which had previously been performed by the local grocer (BMRB, 1963; McClelland, 1962; Sofer, 1965). Food provision was emphasised as an important element in the household's standard of living, an element for which the housewife was responsible.

In many ways, this emphasis on home-centred consumption paralleled the developments of the late nineteenth century and the increasing emphasis given to adopting the 'correct' modes of household consumption and etiquette as a means of enhancing social mobility. The difference was that encouragement to increase consumption in the 1950s and 1960s was also an encouragement for married women to leave rather than restrict themselves to the domestic sphere. The combination of a belief in the primacy of home and family and the need to work was not, and is not, a comfortable combination. The difficulties of the 'dual-role' have, of course, stimulated the development of a market for 'convenience' foods (Tanburn, 1968) and have encouraged retailers to emphasise the 'time-saving' aspects of shopping in supermarkets and planned shopping centres. The difficulties of the dual role have also encouraged part-time work – some of it, as we have seen, in retail shops.

The developments discussed above have not impinged in the same ways on middle-class and on working-class women. For the former, the changes in female employment during the post-war period, while offering many of them jobs and higher household incomes, also involved the loss of servants and delivery services. As Table 4.3 below shows, these changes were reflected in an increase in the time spent by such women on housework in general and on shopping in particular (Gershuny and Thomas, 1983). There was, therefore, during the 1950s and 1960s, a move towards an 'equilisation of drudgery' between the middle- and working-class wife (Wilson, 1980, p. 13). It is true that for both, the use of refrigerators, mechanical kitchen equipment and convenience foods almost certainly led to a more efficient use of shopping and food preparation time. However they also allowed (along with technical innovations in food transport, storage and preparation) an increase in the standard and range of food available and an

expectation of higher standards from the home 'commissariat'
(Dobbs and Hill, 1984). For middle-class married women, there is
little doubt that the whole task of provisioning the home has become
more tiring as much of the labour involved has been transferred
from the sphere of paid work into the domestic sphere. For most
working-class women, while the rise in the standard of meals
expected may have increased the time spent in food preparation, the
time spent shopping probably changed little during the 1950s and
1960s. However, in the late 1970s and more particularly during the
1980s, the growth of superstores and the related increase in the
spatial concentration of food retailing has led to a widening
disparity of access to food retailing services between middle-class
and low-income, working-class women (Bowlby, 1980; CES, 1985).

Table 4.3 *Time spent on shopping: minutes per average day spent by
women aged 25–65, non-employed or working part time*

	1937[a]	1937[b]	1951	1961	1974–5
Working class	16	18	57	54	55
Middle class	40	41	—	47	53

[a]Unweighted.
[b]Weighted to account for sample size. For details of the weighting
procedure and sample see Gershuny and Thomas (1983).
Source: 1937 *Mass Observation Survey*
        1951 *Mass Observation Survey*
        1961 *BBC Audience Research*
        1974–5 *BBC Audience Research*
Data supplied by J. Gershuny, Science Policy Research Unit, England.

Future directions of change in women's social roles and the retailing of food

The discussion in this chapter so far has suggested that during both
the nineteenth century and the recent post-war years technological
and economic change have interacted with existing ideas about
women's domestic role to produce new formulations of what
'nurturing' and 'caring for' a family should entail, and new
conceptions of the ways in which retailing could or should be
organised. While technical changes, such as the freezing of food or
the development of the motor car, opened up new possibilities for

change in retailing methods, social beliefs and patterns of behaviour concerning the role of women in the family conditioned and limited the range of possibilities which were actively considered and developed. Similarly, while factors such as the rise in retail labour costs, and the existence of women as a new, cheap and flexible labour force were of great importance to the growth of self-service trading and the feminisation of the workforce, these factors were themselves partly a result of the socially determined 'need' for women to both service their families' domestic demands and augment the family income.

The past changes that have taken place in the conception and the actuality of women's domestic and wage-earning roles, therefore, have occurred as transformations of older ideas and patterns of behaviour and not as abrupt departures from them. What similiar transformations are likely to occur in the future? How is the ideal and actual relationship between home and work for women and men in different class situations in Britain likely to alter?

Work and the family in the future

One possible scenario is for an intensification of existing class divisions in patterns of waged and domestic work. In a small number of middle-class households both husband and wife would be engaged in well-paid, 'core' employment. The money earned would be sufficient to pay for private child care, domestic appliances and part-time domestic help. In a second group of working-class households both partners would work, but in relatively low-paid and less secure jobs. Their general division of and beliefs about domestic labour would be similar to that of today. However, given the slight trend towards a greater equality in household labour amongst younger couples identified by Gershuny and Thomas (1983), there might be greater sharing of the physical task of shopping, although the decision-making is likely to remain the wife's task (Bowlby, 1984; Scott, 1976). A third group of working-class households, with only a male wage earner, may also be numerically important as a result of a decline in some 'women's jobs' in manufacturing and clerical occupations and the pressure for women with children to return to the home. In these families shopping and other domestic tasks are likely to remain the woman's responsibility. A fourth group which will no doubt also increase is that of households where both partners are not in paid work. In these households there could be a move towards greater equality in sharing household tasks. However, current experience in such households suggests that the problems men experience in coming to terms with not being a 'breadwinner' mean that most are unwilling to undermine their position as 'household head' by doing domestic tasks which they think of as women's work (Allen *et al.*, 1986).

At present competition between food retailers in Britain is fierce and margins are small. Real incomes have been growing slowly in the last ten years and population growth has been negligible. Since only a very small proportion of increases in incomes are spent on food, one of the major difficulties faced by food retailers is expanding demand. As we have seen, this can be attempted by introducing new food products; in addition, overall demand can be increased by diversifying into non-food goods (McGoldrick, 1984). Within this context the current methods for increasing market share used by food retailing companies are to operate larger stores and to differentiate between 'warehouse'-style operations selling goods in bulk with a 'no frills' approach, and more conventional superstores selling both food and non-food items. In both cases the shopper carries out a major part of the labour involved. Retailers have also begun to invest in new computerised methods of recording sales and adding up the bill (Electronic Point of Sale (EPOS) equipment) and, in the near future, it will be possible to make payments through 'Electronic Funds Transfer at Point of Sale' equipment (EFTPOS). These innovations are unlikely to have a major effect on the numbers employed within shops, although they may affect warehousing and bank employment more substantially (Lewis, 1985). Their value to the retailer is likely to be in improving stock handling, providing improved marketing information and in allowing a more rapid throughput of customers.

Experiments in teleshopping, however, suggest more radical changes in the future. Convenience goods could be ordered through an interactive television system and delivered by the retailers (Guy, 1982; Kirby, 1982; Sullivan, 1981). This would substantially reduce the labour of shopping. It would allow greater involvement of husbands and children in shopping without much effort on their part, and could thereby offer food retailers access to an underexploited market. It would also be attractive to shoppers with full-time jobs.

It is uncertain whether the demand for food and convenience goods generated and captured through teleshopping would be sufficient to warrant its cost of investment (Davies and Edyvean, 1984). However, if teleshopping for food (as well as for other goods) is developed, it is probable that it will be directed at, and be particularly attractive to, the more affluent market – the two-earner, middle-class family in particular (Lewis, 1985). This might exacerbate the difference suggested earlier between the domestic labour and employment opportunities of the middle-class 'core' workers and other households. If teleshopping for convenience goods is a commercial success with the most affluent consumers, and as the technology becomes cheaper, we might expect it to be extended to the second group of lower income, two earner households. This would suggest a situation amongst lower income working-class women or single people whereby shopping will remain tiring and time-consuming (or become more so), whilst for the majority of consumers it would become less labour intensive.

If teleshopping for food were to be widely adopted, it would have a substantial effect on the nature of employment in retailing since it would separate the seller and the customer. It might also change the gender composition of the food retail labour force. In existing experimental teleshopping services, men dominate the delivery of goods, but receiving orders, picking and packing goods is more generally done by women. Male dominance in delivery work may result from lower female driving licence holding, coupled with existing social stereotypes about women's suitability for the 'heavy' work of delivery. Female dominance in ordering and packing activities simply reflects their current prevalence in shop work. If such divisions were maintained in the future they would encourage the maintenance of pay differentials between men and women.

Gender divisions in the type of work would also involve gender differences in the location of work. Although the effects of teleshopping on the spatial structure of retailing are disputed (Davies and Edyvean, 1984), it would probably require large, cheap, peripheral sites for regional automated warehouses with smaller distribution depots, near residential areas, from which deliveries would be made. The latter might also operate as small conventional shops and would be where most women would work. Such work locations should be reasonably accessible to women but would tend to restrict their activity spaces while men's delivery work would involve a more active use of space. It is probable that in urban areas some small, family run shops, with long opening hours, would continue to operate to serve those with low incomes and for top-up purchases. Conventional supermarkets would remain for a long time to serve other households. Many might add teleshopping facilities to their existing operations but such adaptations would be unlikely to be competitive with purpose built teleshopping systems.

So far the discussion has emphasised likely trends. However, a feminist analysis must be concerned with identifying ways of changing trends in favour of true equality between women and men. Once we abandon the view that household shopping should be a woman's task it is clear that the majority of potential household shoppers under retirement age are paid workers. If current styles of retailing remain dominant (i.e. self-service supermarkets and superstores), we need to locate shops in places convenient both to people who are not in waged work and also to those who are. One limited short-term strategy would be to locate more food shops on or near industrial estates and peripheral office complexes. It would also mean preserving or expanding some existing town-centre food shops which presently serve many office-based workers but which are under threat from the current trends towards decentralised food shopping. There would still be a place for shops in or convenient to residential areas for use at weekends or on return from work. These locational shifts would not necessarily change the view that food shopping is a woman's task, and could merely make it easier for working women to continue to do the household shopping. However, they could also make it easier for men to play some part – particularly in the present situation where more men than women drive to work and can more easily, therefore, carry goods home.

Such a locational policy would be unlikely to affect the type of shops provided nor would it undermine consumerism. Although it would reduce access problems for workers, it would not eliminate the access problems of the poor, old, housebound or carless. These 'disadvantaged' consumers could be helped by teleshopping technology. Davies and Edyvean (1984) and Lewis (1984) both point to the potential, indicated by the Gateshead Shopping and Information Service, for local authorities to be active participants in the provision of teleshopping services to disadvantaged consumers.

At present food retailing is a largely 'non-political' area – women's work as food shoppers is taken for granted and current trends in food retailing are treated as inevitable developments. There is a need for feminists to challenge this view of food shopping and to debate how the means of purchasing food can best be provided to different households. In the past, feminists suggested that the task of provisioning the home could be changed radically through centralised 'collective' organisation (Hayden, 1982). While different solutions might be put forward today, we also need to bring debate about the provisioning of the home onto the political agenda. This will entail recognising and attempting to change women's current role in the reproduction of labour power, both in the home and in the food retail industry. This role is sustained and encouraged by the current conception of how a woman ought to care and work for her family. This conception will itself undergo pressures for change in the future. Feminists must ensure that some of the pressures for change come from a questioning of both women's roles within the family and the workforce and the organisation of food retailing for private profit.

Notes

1. I would like to thank the editors of this book Jo Foord (London Strategic Policy Unit) and Jane Lewis (Ealing Borough Council) for their very helpful comments on earlier drafts of this paper.
2. *Multiple retailers* or *multiples* are variously defined as store chains with at least two, five or ten outlets. The latter number is the one normally now used in the UK.
3. A *supermarket* can be defined as a self-service store with a sales area of not less that 2000 square feet, selling a range of merchandise covering all food groups, including fresh meat, fruit and vegetables plus basic household requisites. Sometimes the requirement of at least three checkouts is added (McClelland, 1963).
4. *Superstores* are usually defined as 'single-level, self-service stores offering a wide range of food and non-food merchandise, with at least 2500m² (27 000 square feet) net floor space and supported by car parking' (Unit for Retail Planning and Information, 1984, p. 67). *Hypermarkets* are usually defined as superstores with over 5000m² (54 000 square feet) of net floor space (Guy, 1984).

Further reading

Bowlby, S. (1985) 'Shopper's Needs', *Town and Country Planning*, vol. 54 (7), pp. 219–22.
Greater London Council (1986) *Changing Places: Positive Action on Women and Planning* (London: GLC).
Hall, C. (1982) 'The Butcher, the Baker, the Candlestickmaker: The Shop and the Family in the Industrial Revolution', in Whitelegg *et al.* (eds) *The Changing Experience of Women* (Oxford/Milton Keynes: Martin Robertson in association with the Open University).
Murcott, A. (1983) *Eat Up, It's Good For You: Essays on the Sociological Significance of Food* (Aldershot: Gower).
Scott, R. (1976) *The Female Consumer* (London; Associated Business Press).

5

Women with young children: constraints on activities in the urban environment

JACQUELINE TIVERS

Introduction

The study of women with young children gives us an important insight into the nature of women's role in society. As a function of their role women's access to facilities and activities is severely restricted. The gender role constraint acts to restrict the activities of *all* women, whether or not they have children. It is women with young children, however, for whom the constraint is more physically obvious and important, and they therefore form a useful focus for feminist research in geography.

Traditional geographical studies of activity patterns were based within the choice-oriented framework of time-budget research (see Chapin and Logal, 1969; Brail and Chapin, 1973). Hemmens (1970), for instance, wrote that, 'Our analysis of out-of-home activity patterns is being conducted within a framework which views all of the daily activities of an individual as a linked sequence of activity choices.' Any constraints which were recognised (relating to land use and transportation patterns) were seen as implicit assumptions in the formation of choice, rather than as the chief determinants of activity patterns. The same concept of choice mechanisms determining activities is evident in early geographical studies of spatial behaviour; Rushton (1969), for example, stated specifically that 'spatial behaviour, exactly as any other behaviour, is determined by preference only'.

This emphasis on the importance of choice in determining activities has not remained unquestioned. As Pirie (1976, p. 953) remarks, 'Hobson's choice, after all, is no choice, and on many occasions spatial behaviour is rigidly circumscribed'. The notion of *constraints* on activity patterns has been introduced to the geographical literature largely through the work of the time-geography 'school', based originally on research carried out at the University of Lund, Sweden, by Hagerstrand and his colleagues (see Hagerstrand, 1970; Thrift, 1976; Thrift and Pred, 1981). There is an emphasis in time-geography on the modelling of access situations and possibilities. Hagerstrand (1970) stressed that 'access involves . . . a time-space location which really allows the life-path to make the required detours'. Recently, some research has been reported using the time-geographic framework to investigate women's activities (Hanson and Hanson, 1980; Miller, 1982, Pickup, 1983).

Time-geography certainly offers a useful overall perspective on the nature of constraints. In Hagerstrand's terminology, for example, women with young children are subject to many 'authority' constraints since they have very little power in society; they are tied to the needs of their children by 'coupling' constraints, and they are subject to difficulties in movement ('capability' constraints). This approach does not, however, provide the only relevant means of classification; in particular, the complexity of the gender role constraint (see below) seems much greater than the simple idea of having to be at certain places at certain times in order to attend to the needs of children.

The gender role constraint

This chapter concentrates on social rather than on physical, environmental constraints in the study of women's activities. (A fuller account of the research on which this chapter is based is given in Tivers (1985). In considering the constraints operating on the activity patterns of women with young children, it is necessary to look critically at the ways in which society is structured. Physical constraints (mobility and provision constraints) may have an immediate impact on behaviour patterns but they are themselves, with activities, simply the spatial patterns produced by the social processes at work within society. It is argued here that the dominant constraint on women's activities is the gender role constraint, the outward face of the ideology that assigns child-caring responsibility to women. The constraint affects all women, whether or not they actually have children (but to a greater or lesser degree depending on ethnicity and class), because societal expectations about women's 'natural' role influence so many situations. Thus, a young woman straight from school may be considered 'not worth training' for a responsible job, a women with teenage children at school may be 'unreliable' as an employee, and a working wife may not have her income included in mortgage calculations because 'she might have a baby'.

Differentiation of roles on the basis of sex has always been significant and remains so, although variations in its manifestations occur over time and space. The supreme case of an exclusive female attribute is, of course, biological motherhood. However, it is not this biological role which present day society values but the *cultural* motherhood image, encapsulated within the traditional nuclear family. This is reflected in the current political strength of the ideology of the family. Women are confined to the domestic sphere, not on the grounds of sex-discrimination of roles but on the grounds of *gender* differentiation. Despite the existence of considerable evidence to the contrary (see Thompson and Finlayson, 1963; Osborn, 1983), women are constantly subjected to fears that their children will suffer in some indefinable way from 'maternal deprivation' should they seek to pursue activities without them. It is undoubtedly the guilt that women feel, as much as the externally imposed sanctions (although, of course, the two are interconnected), which produces the gender role constraint on activities.

Oakley (1974) makes the point that maternity is a great leveller; most women, whether middle-class graduates or members of the working class, see themselves primarily as wives and mothers. Middle-class attitudes to marriage and family roles have often been seen as 'enlightened' or 'progressive' (as, for example, in Young and Willmott, 1973), but in fact most research evidence shows the middle-class woman to be just as tied to a conventional role as her working-class counterparts. In particular, the wives of managers have their own activities tightly bounded by the work-related social lives of their husbands (see Pahl and Pahl, 1971; Finch, 1983).

It is clear that the gender role constraint is an all-encompassing, and also a relatively enduring, influence on women's activity patterns. However, it is those with young children for whom the constraint is most physically enduring and intense. Women with young children therefore form the focus of concern in this chapter

Other constraints on activities

Although it is true that the gender role constraint is as dominant for middle-class as for working-class women, the ways in which the constraint affects actual activities (especially social activities) differ according to the socio-economic standing of the woman. A woman in a high-income household, for example, may have a living-in nanny to take part-time care of the children and so free her for more varied social activities during the daytime, even though her male partner's position and his demands on her time constrain her ability to work outside the home. The gender role constraint, although still present, may constitute fewer problems for middle-class, higher income mothers; access to a car, in particular, may widen activity patterns without in any way changing the dominance of the overriding constraints. (See the chapter by Pickup in this volume.)

Income and social class constraints on activities are, like the gender role constraint, implicit in the structure of society – and hence 'societal' constraints. It is obvious that a woman will be constrained by the amount of money that she has available to her. Less obvious, perhaps, is the influence of social class norms of behaviour, particularly on social interaction patterns and the use of public spaces such as education/library facilities and recreation areas. Again, as already suggested in relation to the gender role constraint, a woman's perception or interpretation of her role is as important a constraint on activities as any externally imposed restriction.

In the perspective of time-geography, physical and environmental constraints achieve dominance in their effects on activities. However, in this study, it is assumed that such immediate constraints on activity patterns are themselves the products of societal structure, and are thus of less underlying importance than are the gender role and socio-economic constraints referred to above. Nevertheless, there is clearly a relationship between activity patterns and 'physical' constraints, and such constraints should certainly not be ignored.

In the first place, problems of mobility are of extreme importance. Hillman (1970) was the first writer to publicise widely the fairly obvious, but neglected, point that *individual* mobility is not the same thing as *household* mobility. In other words, increasing household car ownership does not necessarily mean that women with young children have greater access to car transport. For women without effective access to a car, different forms of public transportation offer no satisfactory alternative because of the problems of coping with children on buses and trains. For example, Hillman's survey

> shows that women's use of buses is surprisingly low, even for those in households without a car. It indicates that the women prefer instead to use nearby facilities – even if they are smaller; to adjust or delay activities in order to be able to travel by car (if there is one in the household); or to make fewer trips and sometimes to engage in fewer activities. (Hillman *et al.*, 1976, p. 104)

The result of mobility constraints is the propensity of women with young children to make their journeys on foot, and hence to constrain their activities, in spatial terms, to a very limited neighbourhood area.

The other major physical constraint which influences activity patterns relates to the provision of services and facilities, and their spatial distribution: 'at present it is known that territorial inequality is substantial and that men [sic] with the same occupation, income and family characteristics have substantially different life chances in different localities' (Pahl, 1971, pp. 135–6).

One aspect of service provision of great importance to women with young children concerns the supply of child-care facilities. The overall lack of good child-care services is of fundamental importance to the gender division of society, in terms of the allocation of child-rearing tasks to women. Women, to a far greater extent than men, are disadvantaged by both the level of provision and distribution of nurseries, crèches, etc. In particular, in Britain there is a demand for full-time care, which would enable mothers to work, and for greatly increased provision for children under 3.

What is equally clear, however, is that such a demand is very unlikely to be met in the present economic and political climate:

> the implied reasoning [of government] . . . is that, if services are not provided, then mothers will be obliged to stay at home and enjoy their proper role as mother and wife. The main result is, however, that many working mothers have to make child-care arrangements that are not satisfactory for them or their children; they feel guilty and their children may suffer, fulfilling too often the expectation that it is a bad thing for mothers of young children to go to work. (Tizard *et al.*, 1976, p. 145)

Spatial variation in the provision of services and facilities clearly influences activity patterns. As is also the case with respect to shops and leisure facilities, it is notable that work opportunities are most readily available in the inner areas of cities, while outer suburban estates have little to offer in the way of employment (Thorns, 1972; see also, McDowell, 1983). Jobs with associated nursery facilities are exceedingly rare, and the 'coupling' constraint that operates on women, having to take children to a nursery in one place and then travel to another place to work, may make that pattern of activity impossible to undertake (see Lenntorp, 1979). The spatial structure of cities reflects the division between the spheres of production and reproduction, between public and private space, and is thus closely linked to the gender differentiation of society (see chapter by Mackenzie in this volume).

The influence of the gender role constraint on paid employment

In order to study the out-of-home activity patterns of women with young children, and relate these to the existence of different constraints on activities, a survey was carried out of 400 women with children under the age of full-time schooling in the London Borough of Merton (see Tivers, 1985).

The results from the survey (which can only be discussed in outline in this chapter) serve to indicate the overwhelming importance of the presence of young children as a constraint on the activities of women. Perhaps the most obvious way in which this constraint is evident concerns the question of paid employment. Census tabulations for 1971 show that nearly 19 per cent of all women with dependent children under 5 in England and Wales were in waged work, the majority part-time. Within the London Borough of Merton the percentage was slightly higher; here 25 per cent of women with young children were in employment. By comparison, the survey (carried out in 1977) recorded 28.5 per cent of respondents as being in paid employment, almost all part-time.

Clearly, the care of young children precludes paid employment in many instances. This is especially true with respect to very young children. There was, as would be expected, a fairly consistent fall in the percentage of women who were full-time housewives, as the age of the youngest child increased. Commensurate with this decline was an increase in the percentage of women in waged work from 17 per cent of those whose youngest child was under one year old, to 38 per cent of those whose youngest child was 4.

One of the results of societal emphasis on a domestic child-centred role for women is a local, or home-based, orientation of employment. Of the 114 respondents in waged employment, nearly one-third (thirty-seven) worked entirely from home. For many women with young children, paid work in their own home provided the only possible outlet to waged employment. The existence of (often low-paid) homeworking in turn serves to reinforce the home-based and child-centred status of these women, making them subject to a double constraint on activities, since they must care for their children themselves as well as finding time for their waged work duties. In contrast, those who are able to go out to work have freed themselves, at least for some hours a day (or week), from their domestic roles. It must be remembered, however, that this physical freedom from the domestic situation does not also imply freedom from ideological or social constraints. The dual role which many women are forced to carry may be a heavy burden, both physically and emotionally, whether the waged work is undertaken inside or outside the home.

Whereas the majority of employed women worked outside the home, most worked in the immediate vicinity; 37 per cent had a journey of only five minutes or less to get to work, and 70 per cent travelled for no longer than ten minutes. Out of seventy-seven respondents who went out to work only six worked in Central London, compared with 40 per cent of women who were employed there before the birth of their children, and 36 per cent of respondents' husbands. In addition, only nineteen of 292 respondents who intended to go out to work when their children were all at school full time expected to work in Central London, while 220 (75 per cent) intended to work locally and a further twenty-seven said they would probably work at home. These statistics serve to illustrate the deeply ingrained effect of gender role restrictions on employment. Locally based work provides the opportunity for mothers to accompany their children to and from school, and also avoids extensive and time-consuming journeys to work, but it is fairly unlikely to offer the same degree of interest or opportunity for advancement as employment 'up in town'.

Another important result of the gender role constraint is the prevalence of part-time working amongst women with young children. The Merton survey showed only twelve respondents to be employed for thirty or more hours each week. This contrasted markedly with a figure of 92 per cent of respondents working full time before the birth of their children. Nearly half of all those in paid employment worked only in the evenings or at weekends, and the percentage was even higher when only outside workers were taken into account. The accepted principle was that working hours had to fit in with family arrangements. Nor was this a short-term situation; while 80 per cent of respondents stated that they intended to undertake paid employment when all their children were at school, only 19 per cent of future potential workers expected to be employed full time. The influence of the gender role constraint here was very apparent; most women simply did not expect ever to be principal, or even equal, breadwinners for their families. In addition, even when all children were at school full time, there would remain the problem of arranging child care for after-school hours and holidays.

The typical working conditions of women with young children combine to support an ideological belief in the 'peripheral' nature of women's employment. Thus, in answer to the question: Do you think of yourself primarily as a housewife who has a job or as a working woman who also runs a home? only eighteen employed respondents stated that they considered themselves to be primarily 'working women'. Of those respondents working full time, over half thought of themselves first as housewives.

Approximately one-third of full-time housewives in the sample said they would like to engage in waged work if satisfactory domestic and child care arrangements could be made, and two-thirds would in general have preferred to be in waged work, leaving their family circumstances aside. However, paid employment was not the general preference of all respondents, particularly those in higher 'social groups', and there were many women employed at the time of the survey who would have chosen a home-centred life were it not for the financial necessity of working.

The influence of the gender role constraint on non-employment activities

Whether or not they are in paid employment, it is undoubtedly true that women with young children spend much of their waking life 'working'. The unpaid, and largely unrecognised, work that takes place both inside and outside the home is concerned with 'servicing' the family (or the community) (see the chapter by Bondi and Peake). The allocation of this work to women is the result of gender role differentiation in society, and the work itself acts as a constraint on other, 'leisure' and paid employment activities. In addition, the actual accomplishment of unpaid work may itself be subject to the gender role constraint on activities. Perhaps the most informative example to use here concerns shopping for food and household goods.

In the Merton survey, 35 per cent of respondents reported that they went shopping every day, and a further 46 per cent said they shopped two or three times each week. In support of these claims, the time-budget study of the previous day's activities of respondents indicated that 60 per cent of the sample had in fact been shopping on the day before interview. Shopping was clearly a major out-of-home activity for women with young children, but it should not be seen purely as a 'servicing' activity, constraining other, perhaps more desired, types of activity. It is notable, for example, that there was no relationship evident in the data between the age of the youngest child in the family and the frequency of shopping, and in fact women with children at nursery school were *less* likely to shop every day than those with children at home. Children may be a handicap to efficient shopping; nevertheless, shopping may be viewed by many as a way of taking children out and as 'something to do'. This example serves to illustrate the problem of categorising women's activities. However, shopping activity, whether 'chosen' or not, remains a result of the gender role constraint on activities generally, since even in a 'choice' situation it is the presence of children, and their need for care and activities, which determines the woman's behaviour (see the chapter by Pickup in this volume).

In addition, the presence of young children is quite clearly a constraint on actual shopping behaviour. In particular, it determines the location of shops visited; in the survey, 88 per cent of respondents stated that they normally used a shopping centre within ordinary walking distance of their home, and of these more than two-thirds cited travelling problems and other difficulties related to children as reasons for not using bigger centres further afield.

Numerically by far the most important activity outside the home, reported in the time-budget survey of the previous day's activities, involved taking or collecting children to and from school. Like shopping, this is clearly the result of gender role differentiation of activities. The same could also justifiably be said of taking children to parks and playgrounds, and activity that would normally be classified as a 'leisure' pursuit but which clearly is part of the child-care 'work' role. Twenty per cent of the survey respondents stated that they visited a park every day or nearly every day, and a further 27 per cent said that they made a park visit two or three times each week. Of those who visited parks, 80 per cent chose to go to ones with a playground in them, primarily for the sake of their children. It must, however, be remembered that a playground may also act as a social focus for the mothers themselves. For some women with young children, meeting friends in a park may provide a chance for social interaction not obtainable in any other way; this also is a result of the wider differentiation of roles in society on the basis of gender.

The most important 'leisure' activity identified in the survey, in terms of frequency of activity, involved visits to the homes of friends or relatives. It may well be that such activity is emphasised by women with young children, not only because it is enjoyed, but also because of the relative inability of such women to take part in other outside activities. It is also true that home visiting is an activity seen by most as entirely compatible with other aspects of the child-care role. Amongst survey respondents, 62 per cent expected to see friends (and 29 per cent to see relatives) at least twice a week. It is interesting, but perhaps not unexpected (given the importance of societal norms of behaviour), that 85 per cent of respondents cited the fact that they had young children in common as a reason for social contacts with particular friends.

Finally, when asked to consider a range of potential daytime activities, no fewer than 227 respondents (57 per cent) listed constraints relating to child-care commitments as determining their inability to take part in desired activities – especially in the area of adult education and sport.

The influence of other constraints

The major purpose of this chapter has been to exemplify and stress the dominant importance of the gender role constraint on the activity patterns of women with young children. However, within the overall picture of constraint, there are clearly variations in spatial behaviour that can be observed. These variations, in particular, relate to socio-economic differences between respondents and differential personal mobility, as well as the availability of child care on a weekday basis. The influence of these constraints on activities will be briefly discussed.

The provision of state nursery care is obviously insufficient to meet the demands of mothers in paid employment, quite apart from those who would prefer to go out to work if such care were available. As many as 38 per cent of survey respondents who went out to work did not have children at nursery school or playgroups, indicating the lack of fit between nursery school and working hours and locations for a large number of women. It is essential that child-care provision should allow women the choice of whether or not to take paid work, but on the other hand, it must not be thought that all women with young children would prefer to be at work either at the present time, or in general.

Paid employment, so the study showed, was predominantly concentrated in the local area. This was mainly because of the importance of child-care responsibilities, but also reflected the general low level of personal mobility among respondents. So far as other (non-employment) activities were concerned, the main picture that emerged was also of the local orientation of activities. The use of shops and parks near home was the norm.

Approximately one-third of survey respondents had effective access to a car on weekdays (that is, there was a car available for them to use and they were able to drive it), but car availability was not uniformally distributed amongst the sample members; it was strongly related to all socio-economic variables.

Access to a car is potentially very important in alleviating the pressures of the gender role constraint, and it is clear from the survey that higher social class, higher income car users were more satisfied than others with their role as housewives, or if working were more easily able to overcome child-care constraints. This, however, should not be taken to imply that all those with effective access to a car actually used it. While transporting children to school was frequently a car-using activity (indeed, the biggest single number of car trips indicated in the time-budget data were made for the purpose of taking children to school – 35 per cent of all trips), it seems that other activities had a much lower claim on the family car. In many instances, respondents did not feel justified in using the car even for weekly shopping trips, let alone for 'leisure' activities. This clearly reflects the generally low status of the female gender role in society, itself the product of the powerful ideology of the family.

The quality of life

It is impossible to study the daily lives of women with young children without becoming involved in some measure of judgement concerning the 'quality' of their lives, If it can be shown that such women tend to suffer a poor quality of life, then the focus on specific constraints and their remedies is more obviously justifiable. Various attempts have been made to define and measure 'quality of life' (for example, Hall, 1976) using either objective or subjective indicators. Although not without their problems, these approaches have yielded useful information and it therefore seemed appropriate to carry out similar work in the study referred to in this chapter.

Using a semantic differential test comprising a number of bi-polar scales, an attempt was made to indicate respondents' general satisfaction with their lives (for a discussion of the derivation of these scales, see Tivers, 1985). Perhaps the most important result of this work was the finding that respondents generally experienced a low level of life satisfaction (by comparison with other groups studied elsewhere – see Hall, 1976), although those with a very positive attitude to motherhood and also those in higher socio-economic groups had higher overall satisfaction levels.

The quality of life can also be looked at in more objective ways, in terms of actual activity patterns and also the provision of opportunity to undertake activities. It is clear from the time-budget data that respondents' lives were dominated by work (paid and/or unpaid), as might be expected. The extent of social activities was another factor of relevance to life satisfaction, as was the ability to leave children in the care of some other person, at least occasionally.

One cannot leave the subject of the quality of life without noting the presence of very contradictory situations for a number of women in the survey. For women who held positive ('progressive') attitudes, both to employment and to the general position of women in society, actual non-employment status, combined with the presence of considerable constraints on other activities as a result of child-care responsibilities, inevitably led to low levels of satisfaction with life. The incidence of severe depression amongst women with young children has been considered by other researchers (see Brown and Harris, 1978); the data from the Merton survey certainly indicated one possible cause of the problem.

Conclusion

The results of the survey have lent support to many previous research findings and theoretical premises. In particular, the study has illustrated the importance of gender differentiation in society in determining activity patterns. In concluding this chapter it is useful, briefly, to consider whether or not there is any possibility of change in the system of constraints operating on women with young children.

So far as 'physical' constraints are concerned, the likelihood of change occurring seems very limited in a time of severe expenditure cuts on all services in the public sector. It seems unlikely, for example, that public transport services will be significantly improved (except possibly in specific local areas) to ensure greater mobility for daytime users such as women with young children (see the chapter by Pickup in this volume). In any case, it has been demonstrated that greater access to public transport is not a satisfactory solution in itself because of the physical difficulties women face in coping with children. Of much greater significance to the lives of women would be a more adequate provision of child-care facilities, but this too is an extremely unlikely occurrence in the present economic, political and social climate. Political change in the future *might* ensure an expansion of pre-school care, which would have an immediate impact on the way in which the physical aspect of the gender role constraint affects women's activities, but this is by no means guaranteed.

Such an increase in provision would not, however, change the underlying ideology which ascribes child-care responsibilities to women; it would simply shift the problem sideways. A more wide-ranging attack on gender role differentiation, and on the orientation of gender relations which results from the unequal distribution of power between men and women, is necessary before constraints on activities can really be eliminated. Changes in the law relating to discrimination against women are of some help in promoting more 'enlightened' views of the position of women in society, but their importance is limited by the continuing division of labour on the basis of gender.

The acceptance of what has been termed 'androgynous' child care lies at the basis of possibilities for future ideological change. Traditional gender roles will only be revised if social policy (and subsequent legislation) is directed towards helping women and men to develop interrelated roles. However, there is very little sign at present of such a shift in ideology. Increased efforts must therefore be made through education and government policy to free individuals from ideological constraints on behaviour. Real choice can only occur if the whole basis of gender role differentiation in society is re-examined, both at a national and at a personal level.

Further reading

Finch, J. (1983) *Married to the Job: Wives Incorporation in Men's Work* (London: Allen & Unwin).

Hanson, S. and Hanson, P. (1980) 'Gender and Urban Activity Patterns in Uppsala, Sweden', *Geographical Review*, vol. 70, pp. 291–9.

Tivers, J. (1985) *Women Attached: Daily Lives of Women with Young Children* (London: Croom-Helm).

Tizard, J., Moss, P. and Perry, J. (1976) *All Our Children: Pre-school Services in a Changing Society* (London: Temple Smith/New Society).

6

Hard to get around: a study of women's travel mobility

LAURIE PICKUP

Constraints on women's mobility

A concern for travel disadvantaged groups arose during the 'relevance' debate that dominated all aspects of planning activity from the early 1970s and which can be traced back in Britain to the conceptual work of Pahl (1975) and Harvey (1974) or, more specifically in the transport field, to the work of the Independent Commission on Transport (1974) and to the research of Hillman *et al.* (1974). Such work represented a shift in thinking and reflected a growing recognition of the wider social context within which transport operates. A new perspective emerged which saw travel mobility as a special catalyst rather than merely as one influence producing a pattern of 'trips'.

The earliest social studies in transport recognised women as a specific travel disadvantaged group (Hillman *et al.*, 1974). In the most recently published British National Travel Survey conducted in 1978/9 (NTS), only 30 per cent of women held a driving licence compared with 68 per cent of men.[1] Furthermore, among the two-thirds of women residing in car-owning households, evidence from a number of studies shows that women rarely have a car available to use whether they hold a licence or not (see Pickup, 1981). As a consequence of this, women are more reliant than men on public transport to meet their travel requirements.

This situation needs to be set against radical changes that have occurred in women's life-style over the last thirty years or so.

These changes have arisen as a result of the growing participation of married women in the labour market, coupled with a negligible change in the balance of domestic tasks undertaken by partners. Thus working women are increasingly assuming a dual role within society; a role which, it will be shown, involves a complex and intricate scheduling of activities in both time and space.

The growth of married women in the labour market in the post-war period has been rapid. In 1981, 42 per cent of the British workforce were women (Office of Population Censuses and Surveys (OPCS) 1982b). While the numbers of non-married women in waged work fell in all age groups between 1951 and 1981, the numbers of married women in waged work rose in all age groups up to 60 years. Overall, the proportion of married women in waged work roughly doubled between 1951 and 1981 to 56 per cent. This rapid rise has been particularly characterised by a growth in the proportion of married women taking up part-time employment which also doubled between 1951 and 1981 to 50 per cent (OPCS, 1984).

The constraints surrounding the maternal life-cycle have had a major effect on women's labour participation rates. (These changes are discussed more fully in a historical context in Mackenzie's chapter.) Essentially, by extending their control over fertility and childbirth, women have significantly reduced the proportion of adult life spent in maternity and child care. As a result, the female labour force now comprises a full-time workforce of single and middle-aged women and a part-time workforce of mothers with dependent children. Furthermore, evidence from the 1976 *General Household Survey* shows that a high proportion of housewives with young children in Britain would like to return to work if suitable child care facilities existed (OPCS, 1978). (See also the chapter by Tivers in this volume). One-third of housewives questioned said they would work if adequate child care was available. Increasingly, however, the non-waged housewife role is becoming the typical life-style of women between the ages of 20 and 35.

The housewife role has changed with the growth in the numbers of women in waged work, smaller families, new social services and consumer goods. Mackenzie, in Chapter 3, also notes the manner in which housework tasks have changed in past decades. Housework, for most working women, remains a demanding job. However, many of the services which were undertaken in the home are now produced in shops or other facilities away from the home. Thus 'in home' housework time has been partially substituted both into the service sector and into additional travel time necessary to gain access to these services. So despite women's low mobility, it is arguable that their travel requirements are increasing as their dual role develops. In the 1975/6 NTS, while the average daily trip rate for housewives was 2.29 journeys per person per day, the comparative rate among women part-time workers was 30 per cent higher.

In addition, the development of women's dual role has taken place alongside a growing spatial separation of homes and working places in capitalist societies, particularly with, as in Britain and North America, the development of the suburbs. Changes in retail provision have reduced the number of small local stores and supermarkets in favour of larger town centre developments or peripheral hypermarkets (Bowlby, 1978); new schools were also spreading to 'green-fields' sites (Levin and Bruce, 1967). At the same time, the growth in women's employment has not been evenly distributed throughout different sectors but has largely occurred in clerical and service jobs in town centres, and in a mixed market of local white collar or unskilled manual jobs. This degree of sectional and spatial clustering has been less apparent among working men.

Several studies (for example, McDowell, 1981 and other contributors to this book) have argued that the built environment has been slow to respond to spatial implications of a growth in the numbers of working women. By changing the content of their lives, women have placed new demands on the planned environment. For example, the increasing number of mothers in waged work has radically altered patterns of family life, and of social interaction within residential areas. In addition, the previously 'private' domestic role has been partially transformed into the 'public' sphere, changing the travel requirements of women and the timing and location of the journeys they make.

In a number of European countries, recent trends (e.g. suburban growth, rising car ownership, higher costs in the bus industry) have made it difficult to maintain levels of public transport without increased subsidy. In order to reduce government subsidies on public transport, countries have, for example, tied increases to improved productivity (Italy), have taxed local employers to fund public transport (France), or have deregulated commercial bus services to inject free market competition (United Kingdom). In general, subsidies are now being held constant or reduced slightly at the expense of fares rather than service levels. In the United Kingdom, recent deregulation of the bus industry has maintained the overall vehicle miles operated though there has been a reduction in services at 'off peak' times of the day and at weekends. Less well-patronised routes have been cut while services on the most heavily used routes increased. The introduction of minibuses has indeed improved the expansion of bus services into many suburban areas, increasing patronage among the women residents. Given the recent changes in public transport services in Great Britain after fifty years of relative regulation, it is perhaps even more pertinent to ask whether women's increasing travel needs are being met, than it was ten years ago.

In British local planning authorities, methods have been developed in the past decade to identify the 'travel needs' of various population groups including women. In the County and Regional councils, the 1978 Transport Act required authorities to make specific statements on the relationship of travel needs to service levels, which led to the development of a variety of need measurements and accessibility criteria to shops, schools and so on. However, concern with the particular needs of women was not generally explicit in considerations of transport need, rather the emphasis was on the need to maintain access to particular facilities with minimum prescribed levels of services. Following deregulation, these considerations have changed: on commercial services if women have certain travel needs, then it will be in the interests of bus operators in free market competition to provide what the market desires (e.g. minibuses). On non-commercial socially necessary services, local authorities may distribute subsidies according to their own need criteria. It is as yet too early to assess the implications of this legislation on the travel requirements of different groups of women.

While social studies in transport have implicitly assumed that women's low mobility is a product of, and a response to, their social role, few studies have placed an evaluation of their travel circumstances explicitly in this wider context nor taken account of women's changing roles and aspirations. In areas of policy debate outside transport, some feminists have argued that this lack of an explicit recognition of women's social position in research designs has led to a false assessment of their circumstances. Partly in response to this criticism, the rest of this chapter discusses the nature of women's low travel mobility in Britain, its trends and how it relates to their job prospects. It is argued that low travel mobility and women's gender role are inseparably linked. The discussion is based on time-geographic studies of women's activity patterns in Reading, England and analysis of British NTS data (Pickup, 1983).

Types of low travel mobility among women

Rather than the physical frailty or dependency that to some extent defines the transport disadvantage of groups like the elderly or children, it is argued that women's low mobility is a product of their gender role, a role which affects all areas of their lives not merely their travel circumstances.

The role of women within the family cannot be described as a sex-differentiated role since it is not directly related to the function of biological motherhood. Rather the 'female role' is a cultural phenomenon, a result of the gender differentiation of roles, socially ascribed, bearing no necessary relation to the individual's abilities or attributes (Tivers, 1977, p. 87).

There are three types of low mobility that occur among women as a result of their gender role:

1. The impact family-role playing exerts on patterns of women's car availability;
2. The impact of gender-related tasks (both home-based and non-home based) on women's access to opportunities.
3. Low mobility which derives specifically from the conditions under which women travel, the problems of coping with children while travelling and women's fear of sexual assault which deters many from travelling particularly by public transport.

Irrespective of whether domestic tasks are redistributed between household members when women start work, social psychologists (notably Oakley, 1974) have argued that marriage partners still relate to one another along traditional lines. In turn, this pattern is reinforced by the limited types of jobs to which women have access. They essentially occupy a different labour market from that of men, doing jobs of lower pay and quality, often supportive to male roles or merely an extension of domestic tasks (Mackie and Patullo, 1977). Like other areas of women's life-style, the subordinate gender role extends itself to influence the distribution of household travel mobility.

According to the 1975–6 NTS, one-third of women in Britain resided in households without a car. However, of the remaining two-thirds of women residing in car-owning households, 85 per cent lived in households owning one car only. In these households, patterns of car availability and use amongst different members of the household varied considerably. Whilst research by Dix *et al.* (1983) in Coventry has shown that car use decisions between partners in roughly one-third of households were the product of 'objective reasoning' (for example, the journey was impossible using public transport), evidence from elsewhere (reviewed in Pickup, 1981) suggests that such decisions, for a majority of households, were made on the grounds of gender role alone. The general pattern was for husbands to have the first choice of car use, usually for commuting, and for their wives to rely on using public transport or receiving lifts to meet their travel needs. This situation reduced the incentive for women to travel far, particularly if escorting children; it also discouraged women from learning to drive if their access to the car was minimal.

Clearly, there may be a social relationship between the husband's role as chief breadwinner in the family and his priority over the use of the household car. The fact remains that the spatial pattern of men's work journeys are, in general, longer and cover more dispersed locations than do women's. Commuting journeys for at least one-third of men, rely on daily access to a car (Pickup, 1983). However, the pattern of men's commuting journeys is essentially a response to having priority of household car use rather than a reaction to inaccessibility. In addition, decisions on the distribution of car use between household members tend to be made over the longer term when residential locations are chosen. Whilst it is uncertain what influence women's travel needs have on households' residential choices, it is unlikely they would take priority over men's.

Women's domestic role involves activity commitments to which a variety of obligations are attached. While activities like child care and school escort journeys are 'time-fixed' unless delegated to another adult (*hard constraints*), many housework or shopping journeys allow more discretion as to when or where they may be carried out (*soft constraints*). Both types of activity are vital issues in women's job choice. Considerable reallocation, delegation, or loss of tasks is necessary when women consider returning to the labour market; even a part-time job requires reallocation of up to thirty hours of domestic activities each week. Despite this apparent flexibility, the activity patterns of all women, whether employed or not, remain in reality, highly routinised showing little flexibility to change (Cullen and Phelps, 1975). While the relationship between the time spent in child care and employment is strongly inverse for women (Jones *et al.*, 1983), the relationship between domestic 'soft' constraints and their job choices is less clear.

In the home, while many housework activities are easily rescheduled between fixed activities, research has shown that other household activities, like preparing meals, assume the importance of a fixed constraint when women choose jobs (North Tyneside Community Development Project, 1978). Outside the home, women are still primarily responsible for domestic related travel purposes; for example, shopping and school escort journeys. In a study of grocery shopping behaviour in Oxford, 85 per cent of shoppers were women (Bowlby, 1978), while in a survey of school journeys by primary school children in Oxfordshire (Jones, 1977) 71 per cent of children who were escorted to school were escorted by their mothers. In carrying out these activities women may be constrained by a reliance on public transport, cycling and walking, and the requirement upon younger mothers to escort children.

When women consider returning to work, the number of job locations accessible to them is dependent on the time and space conflicts that exist between their gender role activities and available working hours. This point was illustrated by a time-geographic accessibility analysis undertaken in Reading, England, using a sample of eighty-nine job location sites employing 100 or more women (Pickup, 1983). Once the time constraints of working hours were considered, those women with young dependent children were effectively barred from the full-time labour market. Allowing for nursery opening hours, only twenty-one of the eighty-nine job locations were temporarily accessible. Only twenty-five of the eighty-nine job locations operated within school hours and in all cases these jobs were part time. Even within these smaller sets of available part time jobs, the actual number of potentially accessible locations crucially related to residential and job locations and to travel mobility.

So while higher status jobs usually require longer journeys and therefore higher travel mobility (Pickup and Town, 1983), low travel mobility *per se* is of secondary importance relative to the time constraints on gender roles. However, within the limited labour market offered by such time constraints, access to a car is an advantage for reaching a greater range of jobs. In the Reading studies, the few women who did have access to a car travelled more and made longer commuting journeys than women who did not have access to a car.

It is clear that local job choices among women and the locally orientated activity patterns of housewives result from a combination of all of the three aspects of gender-related travel mobility mentioned above, but particularly the activity time constraints. A further analysis in Reading of samples of activity diaries among women in waged work and housewives (Pickup, 1983) showed that child-care commitments and domestic tasks not only affect working status and working hours chosen but also the job locations taken. Classified into seven life-cycle groups, it was women in waged work in those groups with the largest child-care time constraints whose commuting journeys were shortest.

A detailed analysis of British 1975–6 NTS showed that a higher proportion of women than men worked within 1.6 km of home; 44 and 27 per cent of journey to work stages respectively. While a higher proportion of men commuted long journeys, i.e. over 8 km, the proportion of men and women commuting intermediate distances was broadly equal. The NTS shows that, even within occupational groups and at any commuting distance, women's mean weekly incomes were only just over half that of men's. While there was a tendency among all workers for longer commuting journeys to include a larger proportion of higher income workers, as many as 70 per cent of working women commuting between 8 and 16 km to work earned under £2000 p.a. compared with only 20 per cent of men commuting similar distances. This evidence suggests that travel costs, for the majority of women workers, were not an important constraint on job choice; indeed a higher proportion of women than men commute to town centres to work. It was also clear that neither travel mobility nor travel costs, in general, has played a large part in women's decisions to work either full time or part time, indeed the commuting modal split of full- and part-time women workers was similar (see Table 6.1).

When commuting distances were analysed against mean wage levels, the overall spatial wage gradient among women in waged work was less pronounced than that of men. However, there was a steep wage gradient among women commuting to local jobs. The mean income of women commuting between 1.6 and 3.2 km of home was 27 per cent higher than those commuting under 1.6 km. This suggests that, within women's limited labour market, they can substantially improve weekly incomes if able to commute beyond the local job market.

Table 6.1   *Modes of travel to work by men and women (per cent;)*

Travel mode	Car driver	Car passenger Household car	Other car	Bus	Cycle	Walk	Train	Other	Total	Number of respondents
All working women	13	7	5	18	3	48	2	4	100	8486
All working men	39	1	5	9	5	30	2	9	100	12347
Working women:										
Full time	13	8	6	19	2	45	3	4	100	5490
Part time	12	6	4	17	5	52	1	3	100	2922

Source: 1975–6 British NTS Journey Stage data.

Low travel mobility did not have a straightforward impact on the distances women were prepared to commute. The NTS data showed that women's gender role, through its impact on household car availability, affected the proportions of men and women workers who used different commuting modes. However, controlling for travel modes apart from walking, men and women in waged work did not travel different distances in the range within which most job choices occurred. While car use did encourage job choices over a wider area, it did not appear to influence women to choose between local and town centre employment. Rather it was the lack of car use that influenced the set of wider job locations where women did not seek jobs; for example, jobs requiring journeys across suburbs, jobs on the urban fringe and jobs requiring inter-urban travel, i.e. jobs much less accessible to the public transport user.

As well as having poor relative access as a result of activity constraints or low car availability, many women are deterred from travelling due to their perception of the risks involved. Escorting children is particularly difficult for young mothers. While some paratransit services for the disabled admit pregnant women, mothers with prams or folding pushchairs are not permitted, yet they clearly deserve some consideration in this respect. The studies in Reading showed that women having to travel with children did not consider using buses due to the difficulties in coping with them. A study by Hillman *et al.* (1974) in London's Outer Metropolitan Area (OMA) found that the age of children affected the frequency with which mothers used public transport. Housewives whose children were young enough to need prams or pushchairs used the bus on average once a week, whereas mothers with children of 3 to 5 years used buses twice weekly. As well as problems of unreliability, poor frequency and high fares, which were three issues cited by all women bus users, those escorting children also mentioned inadequate routes and long walking distances to bus stops. While better shops or nursery facilities may be available to those using public transport, the added problems of escorting children led to a preference for fewer, more local journeys which is not the case for women car users (Pickup, 1983). Furthermore, recent evidence from France shows that pregnant women who had to commute daily by urban rail into Central Paris suffered a high incidence of premature births due to a combination of the effort involved in climbing stairs and the prolonged vibration on the metro (Pickup and Town, 1983).

The other important aspect of women's travel risk is the fear of sexual harassment or physical assault while travelling. Such fears prevent many women from going out unaccompanied and particular fears exist over the use of public transport – an important point given the economies in staffing that operators are making on their services. To combat these problems, there have been a few experiments to introduce 'safe taxi' schemes for women (Connally, 1982; Pike, 1984) and 'women only' cars have been provided by some metro systems (e.g. Mexico City). The problems posed for women's escorting and safety issues coupled with the reliance many women have on public transport, often restricts them to the immediate local environment which, for housewives, can contribute to the problem of social isolation. The Reading studies showed that, in such circumstances, daily local trips by housewives to shops and schools had an important social function for them in contrast to employed women for whom such journeys tended to be purely functional.

The Reading research identified considerable variation in the attitudes and beliefs of women towards their domestic and working lives and in the perception of their own travel deprivation. These variations can be classified into three different standpoints. In the first case, the housewife role and low travel mobility is an accepted life-style; a choice. If, given domestic duties, a job opportunity accessible in terms of location and hours arises it is taken, and assumes a 'bonus' role in the life-style of the women concerned. In this case travel deprivation is neither felt nor explicitly realised.

The second case most closely approximates to a *constrained choice*. The domestic role is not so much a consciously accepted life-style here, rather it is seen as part of life. Even though they may feel somewhat constrained in their present roles, the women concerned are not aware of the child-care alternatives that might exist; thus they adapt as best they can. Like the first case, any jobs are seen as a bonus and travel deprivation though sometimes felt is not explicitly realised.

The third case assumes that a greater level of *constraint* is recognised by the women concerned. Employment is viewed as a more necessary part of the life-style of these women. Such women faced with using public transport for combining domestic and work roles may be forced into local jobs and may feel this as some degree of travel deprivation.

Discussion – future prospects and policy impacts

Few studies have attempted to assess in detail the reasons for, and the employment consequences of, women's low mobility and the spatial impact of their gender role. The most notable study has been by Hillman *et al.* (1974) in London's outer metropolitan area, but even here the analysis was limited to the study of licence holding and travel patterns. Other early studies, which touched on women's travel patterns, while implicitly recognising the existence of a gender role constraint, paid it little detailed attention. In many ways this led to a false assumption that women, as one transport deprived group, could be catered for by sympathetic transport policies alone. More recently in the transport social sciences, this implicit recognition of women's gender role constraint also occurs in research on travel patterns and the family life-cycle. Unlike the earlier research in transport social sciences where the chief concern was for particular deprived groups, the life-cycle research was more concerned with developing more socially accountable methods of forecasting travel demand. Like other directions in transport modelling, the detailed travel circumstances of women became lost within the concepts of 'household' or 'family life-cycles'. The lack of interest shown in the travel implications of women's gender role may be attributed partly to problems of measurement and of generalisation. However, it should also be stressed that within the traditional 'social variable' type explanations of women's travel patterns, their gender role was accepted as part of normal living (Pickup and Town, 1983). Feminists would argue that it is only when this acceptance of the gender role as normality is questioned that women's problems, including their accessibility issues, are seen in a true light.

The studies undertaken in Reading did show that general statements about the travel context for women's gender role were possible once a time-geographic perspective was adopted. It has been a failure to conceptualise the notions of time and space in women's behaviour patterns properly that has led to problems of theory building in this area of work. Two notable examples of the difficulty of incorporating women's gender role into standard bodies of theory exist. In economics, the growth in women's employment created an urgent need for economic theorists to include household production and consumption in models of employment participation. While it was recognised that time may be the measure of such processes, the subsequent models used the overall amounts of time women spent on domestic activities and valued it at a given fraction of the alternative wage rate. The Reading studies showed that the use of the time concept in these models was crude and that housework time was much more complex in terms of its constraints on job prospects than allowed for in such approaches. The second example related to transport modelling which has been wrestling with notions of the value of time for many years. In the procedures for evaluating expenditure on new or changed road infrastructure, the time-saving for all journeys made other than to and from work is equally valued at one-third the value of commuting time, i.e. leisure activities are valued equally with shopping and escorting children to and from school.

Perhaps the lesson arising from these two examples in labour market economics and planning is that it is difficult to incorporate a rise in women's employment into existing models as they have been developed on notions of society with strict gender role differentiation. Successful incorporation will only occur if theories are rebuilt, 'starting with women themselves' (Tivers, 1976) and this will call for new categories of analysis. For example, theories should include, as a basic premise, the recognition of housework and the reproduction of labour power as 'employment'.

So far in this chapter I have tried to discuss women's travel circumstances in a broader social context than hitherto; their travel issues cannot be analysed in a vacuum. A main issue is whether women perceive travel constraints on job possibilities as a real disadvantage, or whether the ability to combine a domestic and work role is seen as a bonus rather than a right. In other words, do they see themselves as existing in a secondary labour market. If this is the case, the roots of their daily *constraints* may be purely a function of the household *choices* and *trade-offs* they make in the longer term over residential choice or family planning, and we would need to look at such constraints not as essentially transport related but in relation to the broader changing structure of towns and cities.

While many sections of society and government attempt to encourage women to adopt only domestic roles, women themselves attach more and more importance to their role in the labour force (discussed more fully in the chapter by Mackenzie). In communities where domestic and waged work environments are becoming increasingly diverse, the dissatisfaction of women with a limited domestic social environment, coupled with a lack of male involvement in the home, appears to threaten the traditional patriarchal roles of men and women. This is partly reflected by the rising divorce rate, the fall in the number of typical nuclear families and women's increasing demand for jobs (OPCS, 1984). Many tasks women now perform in waged work are essentially extensions of domestic tasks into the 'public' sphere. In turn, the development of women's dual role has led to opportunities for the public sphere to permeate many of the domestic tasks at home, producing a large grey area between the public and private spheres directly attributable to women's changing role (see the chapter by Bondi and Peake).

Both the trends in women's professional employment and the rise of more egalitarian families are long term ones. In Britain, employment trends (Department of Employment, 1982) show that while the proportion of married women in waged work is likely to continue to grow, demographic trends show that the number of middle-aged women in waged work will fall relative to increases in single women and younger mothers. In addition, women will be more susceptible to unemployment in times of economic recession. Joseph (1983) also feels that the impact of new technology is likely to affect women's jobs adversely more than men's, in terms of both jobs lost and the deskilling of existing jobs. However, the number of women in paid employment must not necessarily by seen as a symbol of greater equality between the sexes.

What is to be the response of the transport system to these fairly radical social shifts? Women's travel problems relate to their gender role not to the transport system *per se*. Any policy palliatives to their accessibility problems need to incorporate measures primarily manipulating time use and service availability rather than transport initiatives on their own. The provision of neighbourhood child-care facilities would be one example of such an approach.

Within households, there would appear to be a growing latent demand for car use among wives. For example, one study of car sharing and pooling in Leeds by Woods (1982) found that 45 per cent of all husbands participating in the pooling schemes said their wives used the household car on those weeks when it was available. Furthermore, this sample of husbands included a majority whose wives could not drive thus it could be assumed that among the licence-holding wives, when a car was available it was used. However, these arrangements would still deny women the use of a car for regular commuting needs. While many women do organise lifts to work, the very flexibility in working hours which has provided women with greater job opportunities militates against organising regular lifts. If women are to demand a better matching of working and domestic timetables – their prime constraint – it will inevitably lead to a demand among working mothers for greater parallel flexibility in commuting modes of the sort only private transport can currently offer.

So will car availability among women increase significantly in the future? The trends would appear to be positive; while licence holding among women remains low relative to that amongst men, it has grown from 10 to 30 per cent in eighteen years (Tanner, 1983) and the rate of increase is faster than men in all age groups under 60 years. The proportion of licence holders among women in younger age groups is more than twice that of those in late-middle and in old age. So it may be that, present trends continuing, women's licence holding in Britain will converge with that of men in roughly thirty years. Within this general rise, the apathy among young mothers towards licence acquisition (Hillman *et al.*, 1974) may continue, given their limited car availability, the additional cost of purchasing a second household car and, in many cases, the cost of driving lessons. Clearly, social and ideological barriers still exist between men and women whereby husbands will undermine their wife's ability to drive a car; the mythology of 'women drivers' is well known. Despite these prejudices there has still been a rapid rise in driving licence holding among women, but its future impact may be more significant if car availability becomes a stronger possibility for women in lower social classes whose husbands, so the sociological role-playing literature informs us, hold stronger traditional views on women's social position (see, for example, Oakley, 1974).

For commuting requirements, however, the apathy towards licence acquisition among women as a whole might be lower than among housewives. Indeed, among women in waged work, exerting their greater economic independence, licence holding is higher than among housewives. The proportion of licence holders among women working full time for all age groups under 50 years averages 15 per cent higher than the equivalent proportion of housewives of the same age (Pickup, 1981). So the demands of women's employment do seem to encourage a greater wish for women to learn to drive. What is an important trend is that, with the growth in two car families, women's licence acquisition will be a response to having a car available as a main user rather than as a secondary, occasional user. In the 1978–9 British NTS, roughly one half of all women licence holders had the main use of a car and this proportion had risen from a third since 1965. In future, women in younger age groups owning cars may be much more reluctant to give up their travel mobility after marriage than in past years.

While all the evidence suggests that women's access to cars is likely to increase in coming years, which will both help and be a response to their employment circumstances, the majority of women still cannot drive a car. The fact that an increasing percentage of women now hold a driving licence should not be allowed to detract from the problems of those who do not. In terms of the (private) alternatives to cars, commuters in northern European states where the terrain is relatively flat make greater use of bicycles and mopeds and have more road facilities segregated for their use. In certain areas of Britain where the terrain is amenable, women could make more use of two wheelers (bicycles, scooters, motor-bikes) for their commuting needs, though, on a cautionary note, the safety record of two wheelers relative to other modes implies the need for the provision of more segregated routes to accommodate them.

Beyond the development of greater car sharing between spouses or the purchase of additional cars or two wheelers, the reliance is on public transport; but of what form? Conventional services do provide adequate provision for full- and part-time town centre workers during normal working hours but less so at unsocial hours, on journeys across suburbs, journeys to peripheral workplaces, or journeys between towns. It may be that, other forms of workers' transport services may suffice, perhaps organised by union or employer initiatives. In this way the travel needs of small groups of women workers might be accommodated.

However, there is little incentive for them to provide such services, particularly in times of excess labour supply. It may be, therefore, that women will have to rely on community based initiatives with all the organisational problems involved in setting them up. In this respect, while not being specifically a response to employment situations, the growth in schemes for women's 'safe taxis' is an important step. Primarily to avoid the risks from physical assault, such services operate door to door on a dial-a-ride basis. The one current scheme operating in London was set up by local women in an inner-city district and received a local authority grant to operate for a trial period. Nevertheless, such schemes place local authorities in difficult situations with respect to promoting the merits of public transport as a whole. Safe taxi schemes, it is arguable, might take patronage from public transport. Although the women operating such schemes stress that most of their passengers never went out (often due to bad experiences in the past), they have compromised with the local authority, stating that taxi schemes give women confidence to return to using public transport. In the short to medium term, it is difficult to envisage such travel requirements among women being satisfied by anything other than a door-to-door service. Outside these paratransit schemes which are still at the feasibility stage, the changing pattern of public transport services would not appear to be responding well to the changing travel needs of women in waged work. Early evidence relating to deregulation implies this situation will get worse. The Reading studies did show that a local authority might do better in increasing women's accessibility to jobs by investing in more child-care facilities that in upgrading its public transport network at considerable cost.

Outside the transport arena, planners are also limited in the type of possible response they can make to cushion the impact of low mobility or poor facility provision above what could be achieved by better car-sharing arrangements between households or better child-care provision. Unless improvements in women's travel mobility are accompanied by changes in their child-care time constraints, any transport initiative would have a stifled impact. The accessibility studies in Reading showed that a better co-ordination of times between work, schools and nurseries could improve women's access to jobs. Outside these arrangements, extended families (particularly other mothers and grandmothers) can clearly play an important role in child care in the traditional suburbs to enable young mothers to seek waged work. In new suburbs where such family networks are becoming less common, it has been suggested that forms of community based child care could be a viable alternative to more expensive state provision of nurseries. This may create other problems, however, by reinforcing women's domestic role in the community in a way similar to the effects of caring for the aged in the community (see Ungerson, 1981). While access to shopping facilities may not be a problem for town centre commuters, evidence put forward by Daniels (1980) suggests that women workers in such peripheral locations do face problems and that the provision of local shops or lunchtime shopping buses would be helpful in such situations. This suggests planning a greater mix of domestic, work and school facilities than currently exists in the suburbs.

From the spatial perspective these changes, given women's low mobility, are likely to further increase the demand among women for local employment which the decentralisation of certain types of jobs may satisfy; however, the type of work will continue to be low grade and probably part time. Higher grade jobs for suburban residents still demand a reduction of gender-role constraints, and higher travel mobility of the type many women still lack. It also demands a higher degree of commitment to a career life-style at the expense of domestic commitments, a demand which many women cannot, or prefer not to, meet.

There is pressure for women to broaden their traditional household domestic role to a local community level. This could take the form of local employment in child care and care of the aged, or perhaps local jobs could be provided in areas of new high technology, such as work focusing on remote computer terminals in the home or in neighbourhood work centres. Whether women's social position is to progress in this direction will be open to much debate in future years. Women's service employment in the community would have some advantages for them, enabling them to overcome time-greographic constraints to work, but at the same time the work would remain of a low status and to a large extent would signal women's acceptance of their current inferior social position.

Improving access to employment opportunities among women is neither straightforward nor easily amenable to the direct actions of policy-making. The best prospects for improvement are likely to come via better child-care provision and from more egalitarian households. Part of the answer is how women themselves see their working lives in relation to their domestic role. If there is little career motivation the tendency will be to work locally with little realised travel deprivation. The domestic pressures against women working are strong and involve social issues of more wide-ranging importance than those of just transport. Clearly, however, occupational mobility in many areas requires greater freedom from domestic commitments and greater travel mobility than many women currently possess.

Note

1. Data from the NTS conducted in 1985–6 was not available at the time of writing.

116   *A Study of Women's Travel Mobility*

Further reading

Campagnac, E. and Tabary-Taveau, L. (1981) *Emploi feminin transport et mobilité: l'example de Calais* (Paris: Ministère des Transports DGRST).
Coutras, J. and Fagnani, J. (1980) 'Mobilité quotidienne et mode de vie des femmes en milieu urbaine', *Anal. Espace*, vol. 2, pp. 21–32.
Fox, M. B. (1983) 'Working Women and Travel: the Access of Women to Work and Commuting Facilities', *Journal of the American Planning Association*, vol. 49(2), pp. 165–83.
Greater London Council (1984–7) *Women on the Move* (a series of ten reports, London: London Strategic Policy unit).
Hanson, P. and Hanson, S. (1981) 'The Impact of Married Women's Employment on Household Travel Patterns: a Swedish Example', *Transportation, 9* (Amsterdam), vol. 10(2), pp. 165–83.
Madden, J. F. (1977) 'A Spatial Theory of Sex Discrimination', *Journal of Regional Science*, vol. 17, pp. 369–80.
Schlesinger, G. (1982) 'Working Women's Travel Issues', *Transportation Research Forum Annual Meeting*, 23, 1, pp. 436–42.

7

A means to get out of the house: working-class women, leisure and bingo

RACHAEL DIXEY

Introduction

Despite a vast expansion in literature on the sociology of leisure in an age of supposed 'leisure explosion', research on this topic has largely neglected the particular constraints surrounding women's leisure. With few exceptions feminist academics in Britain have been slow to recognise the importance of inequality in leisure and its relation to other areas of women's oppression. The absence of work in this field is not difficult to understand. In the nineteenth century, women of the middle classes began to make demands for equality with men by demonstrating against their exclusion from the world of paid work and their confinement to the world of non-work or leisure. Exclusion from, and inequalities within, paid work, together with calls to reappraise women's work in the home, have remained central to the women's movement.

In many ways, however, leisure provides a natural arena in which sex role differences and antagonisms can be discussed. Leisure activities are used in the gender socialisation process; throughout childhood sexual identity is gained from particular leisure activities; indeed, there may be as much or even more sexual discrimination in the area of leisure than in any other areas such as work. Thus female engineers and male hairdressers may be more acceptable than female rugby players or male knitters. While it could be argued that the struggle to become an engineer has more tangible benefits than

117

the struggle to play rugby, it is nevertheless the case that enjoyable leisure has an effect on well-being, and that through not participating in certain leisure activities women do not experience the same quality and quantity of leisure as men (see Dixey with Talbot, 1982; Dixey, 1984; Deem, 1982; Gregory, 1982; and Talbot, 1979).

A major problem in attempting to understand women's experience of leisure is that the definitions of leisure found in the literature are couched in masculine terms and indeed, were coined by men. Thus one definition describes leisure as 'a number of occupations in which the individual may indulge of his [sic] own free will . . . after discharging his [sic] professional, family and social duties' (Dumazedier, 1960, p. 2). This definition is inappropriate as a means of describing the experiences of women, particularly those with children, who rarely discharge their family and social duties. Stan Parker (1976) has drawn attention to a number of difficulties in the conceptualisation of women's leisure, placing housewives in a category with the idle rich, the unemployed and prisoners as one in which the divisions between work and leisure are blurred.

Although the leisure studies literature tends to equate leisure with freedom of choice, an attempt will be made here to show that the idea of constraint and lack of choice provides a more realistic starting point when considering women's leisure. It is fairly obvious that those sections of society with limited economic and political power are no more 'free' to choose their leisure activities than they are to 'choose' their housing, jobs, education, the type of medical treatment they receive, etc. Leisure 'choices' are constrained not only by the lack of economic and political power and by what is thought appropriate for each sex, class and age group, but also by the leisure industry, which shapes demand and can restructure or close facilities without reference to the served community. Furthermore, it is often forgotten by researchers that leisure behaviour has already been modified to the limitations of the particular situation. (Thus it may be more revealing and interesting to investigate what people do not do in their 'leisure' time than what they do.)

The aim of this chapter is to look more closely at some of the constraints and limitations that influence the leisure activities of women, focusing on one particular leisure activity, bingo. It is argued that bingo successfully overcomes many of the constraints identified, at least for certain groups of women. The chapter is based largely on a study of women's leisure in the community of Armley in Leeds and also draws on a national survey of bingo players (n = 7166), both undertaken by the author (for further details see Dixey, 1982).[1] Armley, itself, is a predominantly working-class neighbourhood on the outskirts of Leeds – a large industrial city in northern England. Despite its proximity to Leeds, Armley retains a strong community identity, and can trace its history back to the *Doomesday Book*. Economic decline during the 1970s and 1980s has left its mark on the neighbourhood which remains relatively poor. Bingo as a leisure activity featured strongly in the lives of women living in Armley, being played by nearly half of the people questioned in the study. Before considering why this single activity predominated, the chapter will return to examine briefly the major physical and social constraints on the leisure activities of women.

A framework of constraints

In considering leisure within a framework of constraints, spatial constraints are a major consideration; other chapters in this volume by Pickup and Tivers have identified the types of mobility problem that are experienced by many women, particularly those with young children. Not only does a lack of mobility produce ambiguities in relation to leisure, so also does the location of housewives' work in terms of their physical confinement to the home.

Mitchell (1971) has stressed the tripartite role of housewife – childbearer, wife and housekeeper – as the starting point in the analysis of women's position in contemporary society. Housework is seen very differently from other forms of work: 'A schoolboy was recently asked to write down what he thought was the difference between work and non-work. He wrote "Work is what men do. Non-work is what women do"' (Hartnett, 1978, p. 89). The undervaluing of women's domestic work has been described elsewhere in this book, and recognised as a central contradiction in their lives. This contradiction also throws up ambiguities in relation to women's leisure, in a society where leisure is seen not only as the polar opposite of work but is the reward for work. If women's work is non-work then they have no need for the reward for work, leisure.

Women themselves internalise this view: 'In most houses it's the man who goes out to work, and they need their leisure.'[2] Not only does the status of work render the work–leisure dualism ambiguous, but so too does the location of work. As the home is the site for women's work and also of the family's leisure it is less easy for women to 'switch off'. The television as a form of leisure, was criticised by women for this reason: 'Television isn't getting you out of the house. And you're sat watching and you're thinking, "well, I should be doing that", and you feel guilty, you know, you can see it all around you.'

For women without a paid job, 'getting out of the house' is a major need. Men, however, wishing to recover from a day's contact with the world have different needs, as illustrated by this women's remark about her husband: 'When he does come home, I say, "Oh, will you *talk* to me?" and he says, "Oh, I'm sick of talking to people!"' One woman defined leisure as 'anything which takes you out of the house', whilst another woman's husband regarded her part-time job as her leisure as that was the only time she had away from the kids.

While women may be the 'essence of locality' (Hayford, 1974), isolation within the privatised sphere of the home has been described as a major way in which women experience oppression. The separation of residential areas from industrial and commercial areas in modern society, and the resultant decline in importance of the home as a centre of production (and of the status of homeworkers), has resulted in the restriction of many women to the residential environment. This environment is also women's work environment, and the means to move physically from it are limited compared with the mobility of men. Many women are physically restricted to the home, they are actually 'captive wives' (Gavron, 1966). As Peet so aptly remarked, 'Each age group, each social class, each racial group, each sex, has a different sized daily "prism" in which to operate. For the lowest class and the most discriminated against groups, the prism closes into a prison of space and resources' (Peet, 1975, p. 359).

Although Oakley (1974) suggests that the restriction is more psychological than physical, restriction is structured by physical constraints such as the costs of transport, the location of leisure and other facilities, shortage of child-care facilities, the physical lay-out of redeveloped housing and housing estates, and simply by the lack of cash. In a more subtle way, a number of other factors restrict women's capacity for leisure. The ideology of maternal deprivation, fuelled by John Bowlby (1947), has placed greater emphasis than ever before on women's performance as mothers. In the 1970s Comer wrote, 'the hand of motherhood lies heavier on women now than ever before' (1974, p. 191). The centrality of children within the family has perhaps never been so pronounced, whilst support networks for young mothers have never been so fragmented. The erosion of female support networks based on the extended family and higher standards of child care limit the amount of time spent away from children, whilst the physical isolation of young mothers does not bring recuperation in social exchange with others. The trend towards greater consumption of leisure items (drink, video, television games, etc.) in the home means greater blurring of women's time between 'work' and 'leisure', whilst Gavron's study showed that 44 per cent of her sample of working-class women 'never' went out in the evenings. Since her study, there have been moves which have reduced the isolation of mothers with young children. In Armley, for example, there were several new community centres which ran mother and toddler groups, from which friendships between mothers developed. Women, in the way that Mackenzie describes in Chapter 3, were beginning to renegotiate their use of time and space, to find their own solutions to some of the constraints surrounding their daily lives.

These constraints, of lack of time, money, resources, of family commitments and expectations, however, still exist and are summed up in this series of quotations: from the Armley survey

I used to go regularly (to watch football) before I had these two . . . but it's taken for granted that you'll have to stop at home, and any arrangements they've [husbands] made, you have to stop at home.

There's nothing more I'd like to do than to go into town to the pictures, and have a meal, you know, and take one or two of the kids with me but I can't afford it, it's too dear.

I was in the trials for swimming for Great Britian.
Why did you give it up?
Because my dad left my mum and took the car and we didn't have no transport to get to swimming.

You've got housework to do, and your meal to do. You go to bed and you get up and you go to work.

My husband's one of these who doesn't like me going out on my own.

. . . these 'O' level classes I would certainly have taken up by now had it not been that you had to fork out all at one go . . . I can't afford to part with all that at one go . . . we live from one pay time to another.

A major constraint is lack of mobility. One assumption in the leisure studies literature is that, 'car ownership has revolutionised people's use of leisure time' and that 'people have the ability to travel further to better facilities'. The countryside, through the car, has for the city dweller become 'an integral part of his [sic] environment' (Hillman and Whalley, 1972, p. 93). Whilst mobility has obviously increased, it is not spread equally throughout the population (see Pickup's chapter in this volume). Sixty-seven per cent of the women in the Armley sample could not drive and 43 per cent of the households did not own a car. Distance is measured in different ways by people with differential levels of mobility. Thus twenty minutes in a car with children safely strapped in the back is translated into perhaps one and a half hours for the woman on public transport, with the cost of fares, changes of bus, waiting time, and the difficulties of boarding children and push chairs to take into account. The usual way for women to get around is to walk. One woman explained why she wasn't interested in a keep-fit class:

'You see I walk to school in the mornings, then I walk home again. Then I walk to pick him up and then I walk home again, then I walk up to the school to pick her up and then I've to walk home again. So I do enough without any more . . .'

People in Armley have seen local leisure facilities close in the same way that they have seen local factories close; women never knew whether their husbands might be laid off, temporarily or permanently, and in such an environment, lack of control over leisure facilities is simply seen as part of a larger powerlessness.

The loss of local facilities is related to the physical disruption of working-class neighbourhoods which has taken place in the past few decades. The most visible changes faced by the working class in recent times are the vast rehousing schemes that disrupted the homogeneity and cohesiveness of the community by moving people out to new housing estates or to high rise flats. Although it is now recognised that it is better to rebuild on the same sites, physical restructuring is still disruptive and tends to result in a reduction of semi-public space. This is amply documented by Cohen (1972). Replacing the old communal street, with its pub and corner shops, 'there was only the privatised space of the family unit, stacked one on top of the other, in total isolation, juxtaposed with the totally public space which surrounds it' (Cohen, 1978, p. 16). Semi-public space in which interaction could take place was lacking and the social costs were high. Moreover, the semi-public (masculine) spaces of pubs and clubs were still denied to women in their own right. This is where bingo appears.

At the simplest level, it can be argued that the bingo club provides for women the right kind of setting for the non-intimate companionship which characterises the working-class community. During the course of the research, bingo was often referred to as the only place where women could walk in on their own and feel comfortable:

I've got three kids and I've nowhere else to go.

It's the only thing I get to do.

Well there aren't a lot of facilities for leisure – there's bingo . . .

I mean if you don't play bingo, there's not much, there's few picture houses now . . .

I was going out of my head living in the flat 'cos I was stuck there all day on my own and it (bingo) was the only way I'd get out of the flat. (Old lady)

The role of bingo

At this point it is perhaps useful to make a few comments on the development of bingo. These can be summarised in the following four points:

1. It was the 1960 Betting and Gaming Act that made commercial bingo legal.
2. Large numbers of people play; after the extraordinary success of the game in the early 1960s (by 1966 24 per cent of the population took part in commercially organised bingo), numbers reached a plateau by the early 1970s and now the industry is concerned about a relative decline.
3. It is a profitable business dominated by a small number of large companies which also have other leisure interests.
4. The Gaming Board has a large say in the form bingo takes.[3] It wishes to emphasise the social side of the game, to keep it firmly separated from gaming. It adopts a somewhat paternalistic stance, 'saving' women from exploitation.'

These points may imply that in 1960 bingo was 'new', and in some respects it was. However, it is possible to see bingo as representing a historical continuity in terms of three factors. First, working-class female gambling; women are certainly not new to gambling. Secondly, the commercial provision of leisure, dating from 1884 and the establishment of Mecca, when working-class games and past-times had been restructured by urbanisation and industrialisation and people became consumers, not producers of leisure. Thirdly, the game itself is not new. Forms of games with numbers go back at least to the sixteenth century. The way games are structured reflects the society in which they are found; thus, in a capitalist society bingo is structured to produce profit.

Six million people play bingo regularly in Britain at 1600 commercial bingo clubs is slightly less than half a million, Bingo is (according to Gaming Board figures). Daily attendance at commercial bingo clubs is slightly less han half a million. Bingo is also played at other venues – social clubs, church halls, and community centres for which figures are not available. In Armley bingo was played by 47 per cent of the sample of women at five different types of venue. Armley is predominantly working class and bingo is a predominantly working-class game. Given the social and occupational structure of the community and the lack of alternative facilities available, it is perhaps not surprising that nearly half the sample played bingo. (It is interesting to note that class barriers are more important than those of gender as bingo more effectively excludes the middle class as a working-class game than it does men as a female game.) In the national sample 16 per cent of players were men but only 8 per cent were white collar or professional workers.

In view of the constraints operating on women it is easy to see why they play bingo. It is relatively cheap (the usual amount spent in 1981 was £3 per evening or afternoon), it does not take up too much time, it requires no particular commitment, it is acceptable to husbands and venues tend to be local and handy. For most (as most do not play on the fruit machines or interval games), bingo is not a gamble in that it is known exactly how much will be spent at each session. Ninety-five per cent of the players played at least once a week, and 77 per cent twice a week. Apart from these mainly superficial reasons, the explanations for the success of bingo can be located in the nature of women's roles, the form of the working-class community and the control of leisure provision by the leisure industry.

For women in Armley, bingo was the most frequent leisure activity outside the home, apart from going to the pub. The national survey found that bingo was the main leisure activity outside the home for 71 per cent of the sample; this was so for 51 per cent of the 26–35 age group and for 89 per cent of the 76 plus age group. Women did not feel at ease going unescorted into the masculine environment of the pub, and none of the women interviewed in Armley would go into pubs alone. Just as pubs provide a kind of 'home from home' for men, remarks made by women in the course of fieldwork suggest that to them the bingo club is a 'home from home'. Many women, particularly the older ones, would arrive up to two hours before the game started, to eat, talk, knit, read or play cards with others. Some even said that they felt happier at the bingo than at home, where all too often they would be alone. One club even opened on Christmas Day for those with nowhere else to go.

The feeling of ease and familiarity in the bingo club is facilitated not only by the club being an extension of the community, but also by the fact that clubs have usually been physically present in the community for many years, as cinemas and later as bingo clubs. The similarity between the use of the cinema in the 1940s and the use of the bingo club since the 1960s is striking. Kuper writing in the early 1950s remarks:

It is not at all unusual for women to attend the cinema unaccompanied. For many women with young children the cinema is the sole relaxation outside the home and they often come alone while the husband looks after the family . . . Going to a show is an occasion for active neighbouring; it expresses an established relationship and provides the opportunity for greater intimacy. As for the men, the cinema has little effect (Kuper, 1953, p. 120).

Whilst playing bingo replaced watching films in cinemas, the way in which the two activities are used is remarkably similar. The custom of women going unaccompanied to the cinema may help to explain why men readily accept their wives going to bingo unaccompanied.

The bingo club therefore plays a vital role in providing a semi-public space which is local and handy, and, as an extension of the community, brings feelings of rootedness and 'at-homeness'. Moreover,

Bingo is one of the easiest places to start to be sociable

You don't notice one person coming in on her own to bingo.

I know I'm not going to get accosted by a perfect stranger . . . a lot of women think the same because you get a lot of women going in on their own . . . you can drink and you can have a laugh and you're safe.

It is the 'femaleness' of the club that renders it acceptable to husbands, whilst often it is contact with other women *per se* which is sought; 'The reason I come in the afternoon is to get other women to talk to. I've got two sons and a husband at home, and well, men don't talk as much as women do.' The club can provide an opportunity for female family members to meet, particularly if they live in different parts of the area: 'My night out is Wednesday and I have to come to bingo – well I don't have to come, but I come to the bingo and I meet my friends, and my sister, my relations and that.' In this predominantly female environment, women not only feel free from unwanted contact with men, but also any sexual innuendo is under their control (jokes directed at the male caller for example) and for once, not directed at them.

For a minority of players bingo clubs provide their only source of companionship. This minority comprises mainly older players who do not belong to the church or other organisations and who do not see family members on a regular basis. Comments from elderly people such as, 'Bingo is my lifeline' and 'Bingo is the only thing that keeps me going', were frequently heard, whilst a handful of older women were most concerned that the aim of the research was to 'close down bingo clubs' – 'You're not going to take it away are you? It's all we've got.' In this sense it can be argued that the bingo club provides a valuable social network in an age when other social and caring networks have failed. A report prepared for the DHSS in 1981 declared that the government's attempts to provide a system of voluntary care in Britain, rather than investing in paid community care, had failed: 'Those most in need – the old with no relatives – were largely ignored in urban areas unless there were paid social workers to watch over their welfare' (*The Guardian*, 15 September 1982, p. 2).

Some younger women enjoyed playing on their own, sitting, not having to talk to anyone. For them bingo provides a useful break from the children rather than a social occasion. Other women set aside their 'bingo time' as the time which was theirs, away from home, with their own friends. The number of references to 'regaining sanity', or 'a bit of peace and quiet' reflects the strains imposed on mothers with young children. Twenty-two per cent of the players had children under the age of 16; the average age for women to take up bingo was 38, but 17 per cent of the players were aged less than 35.

The fact that bingo is a home-from-home for many (but not all) players, has implications for behaviour inside the club. The notion of 'at homeness' has a reverse side, that of feelings of territoriality which comprise aggression. Territoriality involves the organisation of space into 'Clearly demarcated territories which are made distinctive and considered at least partially exclusive by their occupants' (Soja, 1971, p. 19). Thus inside the club, individuals or groups 'always' sit in certain seats, and their right to sit there is defended; 76 per cent of the national sample like to sit in the same seat. Bingo players in Armley referred in effect to the defence of space, that having their 'own' seat allowed them greater control over their choice of neighbours. The following conversation with a 36-year-old female respondent illustrates this point.

INTERVIEWER   Do you always sit in the same bit?

RESPONDENT   Yes, my own seat. It's almost got my name on.

INTERVIEWER   The seat I saw you on?

RESPONDENT   Yes, that is my seat and I always sit on it. It's very, very rare that I sit anywhere else and if I do it's only one or two rows away from it, if someone else is sitting in it.

INTERVIEWER   Do you mind that?

RESPONDENT   Not particularly. It's not my seat as such, it's just that I like to sit round about there.

INTERVIEWER   Why do people have special seats?

RESPONDENT   I've no idea, because I didn't used to have. I sat there a couple of times and another couple I know sat in front of me. If I wasn't there they started saving that seat for me. So now it's automatic that I do sit there. I don't know why because it's not at all comfortable.

INTERVIEWER   They're not, are they, those cinema seats?

RESPONDENT   The table's more comfortable, but you can't occupy a table all to yourself. If you want to be on your own, you can sit in those seats and put your bags down and such, so that no-one will come and sit with you, but at a table you'd always get somebody pestering you.

That people have their 'own' seats can cause friction. One manageress recalls being called to a dispute one evening where another women was sitting in a regular player's seat. Rather than take another seat in the near empty club, the regular player went home. One respondent commented

> You do tend to find that if you go for the first time and you want to sit in a seat that somebody else has sat in for years, you can cause a big argument. There are signs up saying that no seats are reserved but that doesn't seem to follow. People do moan if you happen to sit in their seats. Its the older generation that do that.

Arriving early and sitting in a particular seat allows the player greater control over whatever social interaction takes place: 'It opens at half past six and if I go I've to go at half past five to get a seat, because if you go a bit late you have to squash in with somebody.' If bingo is used to maintain kinship and social networks in the community, it is essential that there are 'rules of contact' inside the club. Knowing with whom one will interact is also an important feature of the *ritual* of bingo. If ritual is activity which expresses a 'striking or incongruous rigidity . . . some conscious regularity' (Nadel, 1954, p. 159) then bingo can correctly be called a ritual. Goody (1961), however, points out that the description of action as ritual or the attribution of 'symbolic' elements to action is often a way of announcing that the researcher is unable to make any sense of the observed action or behaviour.

The routine of bingo is not resisted. Rather, people create their own precise routines which fit into the already highly structured game. People arrive at a certain time each week; managers can recite the times at which regular players always arrive. One player comments:

> Yes, yes. As I say, it's routine; you know exactly what's going to happen. What time this is going to finish and what time that is going to finish. You can sort of plan your night out you know, because you know there won't be any change unless something drastic happens, of course, but you don't think of things like that.

The regularity of involvement in particular activities was noted in the leisure lives of people of Armley, whilst bingo players had some interesting thoughts on why they enjoyed the routine of bingo:

INTERVIEWER Why do you think people have such a routine in bingo?

RESPONDENT I've no idea . . . I think we're all creatures of habit. I think you're just brought up from the cradle so that you do certain things at certain times and you're secure in a routine. I mean, with little kids, the ones that cry and carry on are the ones with no routine, whereas if you know what's coming next you feel a lot safer.

I think people feel safe. I think people get frightened at too much change . . . I think people are a bit frightened if things are altered too much. People tend to just want to stay as they are.'

Other researchers have noted that the most popular leisure activities in certain communities are repetitive. Men in the pub and women at bingo sit in the same places and meet the same people on the same nights each week. It is suggested that reassurance arises from repetitive activities and from spending time in familiar haunts and with familiar people and through playing familiar roles. It has also been suggested that the working classes have a greater need to play familiar roles than the middle classes. Harrison notes the 'fundamental uncertainty' of working-class life, and that working-class families are more exposed to disaster than the middle class (Harrison, 1975). Likewise, Fyvel, (1963) noted that the working class is more vulnerable to the socially and psychologically harmful effects of rehousing and the break up of community life. This kind of argument, however, verges on the pathological explanations commonly found in the press rather than on a materialist explanation.

Conclusion

In the 1980s, the recession has speeded up rather than caused the relative decline in bingo playing, first observed in the 1970s. Naturally the bingo industry has expressed concern (in 1982 the National Association of Licensed Bingo and Social Clubs launched a 'Survive and Thrive' campaign). Also, although bingo is still a popular pastime – clubs attract between one-third and half a million people every day – there is evidence to suggest that many women would prefer to engage in other activities if they had the opportunity, and that bingo is played not as a positive choice but due to a lack of alternatives. Dobbin (1980) provides useful data by showing that, of his sample of retired people, bingo ranked fourth in a list of ten activities that respondents most often engaged in, but ranked last in a list of activities in which they would like to be more involved. As Cornish (1978, p. 361) points out:

> The presence of institutionalised expressive activities in a culture does not necessarily imply that they owe their existence to their superior ability at meeting special expressive needs . . . for each new generation the satisfactoriness of these contingent arrangements is once more on trial.

If bingo does not owe its existence to the fact that it is the best way of satisfying people's (especially women's) demands for entertainment and excitement, it is still the only form of leisure outside the home available to large numbers of people – especially women – at present.

Large groups of people, and particulary women, remain unaffected by the 'leisure explosion' and by the expansion of leisure-time choices. In the 1980s, an estimated 15 million people in Britain live in 'poverty' (Brown and Madge, 1982) and 1.8 million live in physically unsatisfactory housing. One-quarter of all households consist of elderly people, many of whom have limited financial means, and three-quarters of whom left school at 14 without qualifications. A leisure future conjured up by futurologists in which 'only a small percentage of people work . . . while the rest of us get on with home computing, Open University degrees, learning foreign languages and other edifying pursuits' (*The Observer*, 4 July 1982, p. 25) will be available only to a small minority. The need for cheap, sociable entertainment outside the home in the 1980s has not diminished. Alternatives to bingo, however, have not been established.

The significance of bingo lies not in the game itself. Rather, bingo is a cypher to which different groups attach meaning and content. To members of the middle and upper classes it may still be pernicious, symbolic of the decadence and apocalyptic powers of popular culture. Commenting on a recent radio programme, a reviewer wrote: ' "God knows what we'd do if we didn't go to bingo," said one hooked lady. And that's surely a sad comment on our education system' (*Radio Times*, 11 September 1982, p. 42).

To the government, bingo represents a substantial source of revenue. Further, it can be argued that bingo saves the government expenditure on community care. Bingo provides a living for large numbers of people, not only for the owners of Britain's 1600 clubs and their 2019 managers, but also for the several tens of thousands of staff employed.

To the players, bingo is an unremarkable fact of life, a home from home, an invaluable source of companionship, a refuge which offers excitement. It is not surprising that 84 per cent of players are women, given the options bestowed on them by virtue of their gender. The future of bingo is dependent not only on changes in the leisure market and in the state of the economy but also on changes in gender roles. For the present, bingo is an activity adopted and fashioned within the limitations of an imposed structure by those not in an economically, politically or socially dominant position. Bingo is used to give expression and meaning to that position; it is also a most important means of coming to terms with that position and making it more attractive.

Notes

1. The community study was carried out over a year and comprised in-depth recorded interviews with sixty-eight women, a lengthy questionnaire to 200 women plus 'participant observation'. The national survey comprised a questionnaire completed by 7166 respondents in bingo clubs throughout the country.
2. Unreferenced quotations are from women who took part in the study.
3. The Gaming Board was established as a result of the 1968 Gaming Act in order to perform a 'watchdog' role, i.e. to ensure that the regulations and procedures embodied in the act were adhered to.

Further reading

Clarke, J. and Critcher, C. (1985) *The Devil Makes Work: Leisure in Capitalist Britain* (London: Macmillan).

Deem, R. (1986) *All Work and No Play? The Sociology of Women and Leisure* (Milton Keynes: The Open University).

Dixey, R. with Talbot, M. (1982) *Women, Leisure and Bingo* (Horsforth, Leeds: Trinity and All Saints College).

Rojeck, C. (1985) *Capitalism and Leisure Theory* (London: Tavistock).

Bibliography

Ahonen, P. H. (1981) *Variations in Leisure Activities: Realities and Perceptions of Married Women*, Paper presented at the 3rd Canadian Congress on Leisure Research (Alberta: University of Alberta).

Alexander, D. (1970) *Retailing in England During the Industrial Revolution* (London: Athlone Press).

Alexander, S. (1976) 'Women's Work in Nineteenth Century London: A Study of the Years 1820–1850', in Mitchell, J. and Oakley, A. (eds) *The Rights and Wrongs of Women* (Harmondsworth: Penguin).

Allen, S., Watson, A., Purcell, K. and Wood, S. (eds) (1986) *The Experience of Unemployment: Explorations in Sociology, 21* (London: Macmillan).

Amos, V. and Parmar, P. (1984) 'Challenging Imperial Feminism', *Feminist Review*, vol. 17, pp. 3–19.

Anthias, F. and Yuval-Davis, N. (1983) 'Contextualising Feminism – Gender, Ethnic and Class Division'. *Feminist Review*, vol. 15, pp. 62–75.

Antipode (1984) Special issue on 'Women and the Built Environment' vol. 16(3).

Auld Committee (1984) *The Shops Act: Late Night and Sunday Opening: Report of the Committee of Inquiry into Proposals to Amend The Shops Act*, Chairman Robin Auld, Cmnd 9376 (London: HMSO).

Austerberry, H. and Watson, H. (1981) 'A Woman's Place: A Feminist Approach to Housing in Britain'. *Feminist Review*, vol. 8, pp. 49–62.

Barrett, M. (1980) *Women's Oppression Today* (London: Verso).

Bazen, S. (1985) *Low Wages, Family Circumstances and Minimum Wage Legislation* (London: Policy Studies Institute).

Beechey, V. (1977) 'Some Notes on Female Wage Labour in Capitalist Production', *Capital and Class*, vol. 3, pp. 45–66.

Bell, C. and Newby, H. (1976) 'Community, Communion, Class and Community Action: The Social Sources of the New Urban Politics', in Herbert, D. and Johnston, R. (eds) *Social Areas in Cities* (London: John Wiley).

Bell, D. (1973) *The Coming of Post Industrial Society* (New York: Basic Books).

Bleitrarch, D. and Chenis, A. (1981) 'Modes of Domination and Every Day Life: Some Notes on Recent Research', in Harloe, M. and Lebas, E. (eds) *City, Class and Capital* (London: Edward Arnold).

Bowlby, J. (1947) *Child Care and the Growth of Love* (London: Harmondsworth).

133

Bowlby, S. R. (1978) 'Accessibility, Shopping Provision and Mobility, in Kirby, A. and Goodall, B. (eds) *Resources in Planning* (London: Pergamon Press).

Bowlby, S. R. (1980) *Mobility and Information: A Study of Knowledge of Grocery Shopping Opportunities*. Final report to the Social Science Research Council, Grant no. HR3379/2.

Bowlby, S. R. (1984) 'Planning for Women to Shop in Post-war Britain', *Environment and Planning D: Society and Space*, vol. 2, pp. 179–99.

Bowlby, S. R. (1985) 'Shopper's Needs', *Town and Country Planning*, vol. 54(7), pp. 219–22.

Bowlby, S. R., Foord, J. and Mackenzie, S. (1982) 'Feminism and Geography, *Area*, vol. 14, pp. 19–25.

Bowlby, S. R., Foord, J. and McDowell, L. (1986) 'The Place of Gender in Locality Studies', *Area*, vol. 18(4), pp. 327–31.

Brail, R. K. and Chapin, F. S. (1973) 'Activity Patterns of Urban Residents', *Environment and Behavior*, vol. 4, pp. 163–90.

Brason, N. and Heinemann, M. (1973) *Britain in the Nineteen Thirties* (St Albans: Panther).

Brenner, J. and Ramas, M. (1984) 'Rethinking Women's Oppression', *New Left Review*, vol. 144, pp. 33–71.

British Market Research Bureau (1963) *Shopping in Suburbia* (London: BMRB).

Brittain, V. (1979) *Testament of Youth: An Autobiographical Study of the Years 1900–1925* (London: Fontana/Virago).

Brooks, E. (1973) *This Crowded Kingdom: An essay on Population Pressure in Great Britain* (London: Charles Knight).

Brown, C. (1984) *Black and White in Britain: The Third PSI Survey* (London: Heinemann).

Brown, G. W. and Harris, T. (1978) *Social Origins of Depression: A Study of Psychiatric Disorder in Women* (Andover: Tavistock).

Brown, M. and Madge, N. (1982) *Despite the Welfare State* (London: Heinemann Education).

Bryan, B., Dadzie, S. and Scarfe, I. (1985) *The Heart of the Race* (London: Virago).

Built Environment (1984) Special issue on 'Women and the Built Environment, vol. 10(1).

Button, S. (1984) Women's Committees, *School for Advanced Urban Studies, Working Paper 45* (Bristol: SAUS).

Campagnac, E. and Tabary-Taveau, L. (1981) *Emploi feminin, transport et mobilité: l'example de Calais* (Paris: Ministère des Transports, DGRST).

Campbell, B. (1984) *Wigan Pier Revisited* (London: Virago).

Campbell, B. (1987) *Iron Ladies* (London: Virago).

Campbell, B. and Lovenduski, J. (1987) 'Whats in it for women?' *The Guardian*, 2 June, p. 24.

Carby, H. (1982) 'White Women Listen! Black Feminism and the Boundaries of Sisterhood', in Centre for Contemporary Cultural Studies. *The Empire Strikes Back: Race and Racism in the 1970's Britain* (London: Hutchinson).

Castells, M. (1976) 'Is There an Urban Sociology?' in Pickvance, C. (ed.) *Urban Society: Critical Essays* (London: Methuen).

Castells, M. (1977) *The Urban Question* London: Edward Arnold).

Castells, M. (1978) *City Class and Power* (London: Macmillan).

Castells, M. (1983) *The City and The Grassroots* (London: Edward Arnold).

Central Statistical Office (1972) *Social Trends* (London: HMSO).

Centre for Environmental Studies (1985) *Access to Food Stores in London: A Pilot Study of Three Large Retailers* (5 Tavistock Place, London: CES

Chapin, F. S. and Logan, T. H. (1969) 'Patterns of Time and Space Use', in Perloff, H. S. (ed.) *The Quality of the Urban Environment: Essays on 'New Resources' in an Urban Age* (Washington DC: Resources for the Future, Inc).

Clark, A. (1968) *Working Life of Women in the Seventeenth Century* (London: Frank Case (originally published 1919)).

Clarke, J. and Critcher, C. (1985) *The Devil Makes Work: Leisure in Capitalist Britain* (London: Macmillan).

Cockburn, C. (1977a) *The Local State* (London: Pluto Press).

Cockburn, C. (1977b) 'When Women Get Involved in Community Action', in Mayo, M. (ed.) *Women in the Community* (London: Routledge & Kegan Paul).

Cohen, P. (1972) Sub-cultural Conflict and Working Class Community *Papers in Cultural Studies*, 2, pp. 5–51 (Centre for Contemporary Cultural Studies, University of Birmingham).

Cohen, P. (1978) *Subcultural Conflict and Working Class Community*. Working Papers in Cultural Studies, 2.

Conference of Socialist Economists, London Edinburgh Weekend Return Group (1980) *In and Against the State* (London: Pluto Press).

Comer, L. (1974) *Wedlocked Women,* (London: Feminist Books).

Connally, J. (1982) *Ann Arbour Takes a Night Ride*, Ann Arbour Transportation Authority UC/PT1 Transportation Project, 738 (Ann Arbor: AATA).

Cornish, D. B. (1978) *Gambling: A Review of the Literature* (London: HMSO).

Counter Informaton Services (1976) *Women Under Attack,* Anti-Report no. 15 (London: CIS).

Counter Information Services (1981) *Women in the 1980s* (London: CIS).

Coutras, J. and Fagnani, J. (1980) *Obilité quotidienne et mode de vie des femmes en milieu urbaine*, Organisation Rapport du Société de Mathematique Appiquées et des Sciences Humaines, Paris. Delegation Géneralé a là Recherche Scientifique et Technique (DGRST).

Coward, R. (1984) *Female Desire: Women's Sexuality Today* (London: Paladin).

Crine, S. (1979) *The Hidden Army*, Low Pay Pamphlet, no. 11 (London: Low Pay Unit).

Cullen, I. and Phelps, E. (1975) *Diary Techniques and the Problems of Urban Life*. Final report to the Social Science Research Council, Grant no. HR2336.

Currie, D. and Kazi, H. (1987) 'Academic Feminism and the Process of De-radicalisation: Re-examining the Issues', *Feminist Review*, vol. 25, pp. 77–98.

Daniels, P. W. (1980) *Office Location and the Journey to Work: A Comparative Study of Five Urban Areas* (Farnborough: Gower).

David, M. (1983) 'Sex Education and Social Policy: A New Moral Economy', in Walker, S. and Barton, L. (eds) *Gender, Class and Education* (Lewes: Falmer).

Davidoff, L., L'Esperance, J. and Newby, H. (1976) 'Landscape With Figures: Home and Community in English Society', in Mitchell, J. (ed.) *The Rights and Wrongs of Women*, (Harmondsworth: Penguin).

Davies, C. S., Fowler, G. L. (1971) 'The Disadvantaged Black Female Household Head: Migrants to Indianapolis', *Southeastern Geographer*, vol. 11, pp. 113–20.

Davies, R. L. and Edyvean, D. J. (1984) 'The Development of Teleshopping', *The Planner*, August, pp. 8–10.

Davis, D. (1966) *A History of Shopping* (London: Routledge & Kegan Paul).

Deem, R. (1982) 'Women, Leisure and Inequality', *Leisure Studies*, vol. 1 (1), pp. 29–46.

Deem, R. (1986) *All Work and No Play? The Sociology of Women and Leisure* (Milton Keynes: Open University).

Department of Employment (1982) 'Forward Look – Mobility Within Local Labour Markets', *Department of Employment, Research Paper, No. 24* (London: HMSO).

Department of Transport (1979) *National Travel Survey: 1975/6 Report* (London: HMSO).

Department of Transport (1983) *National Travel Survey: 1978/9 Report* (London: HMSO).

Dix, M. C., Carpenter, S., Clarke, M. I., Pollard, J. and Spencer, M. (1983) *Car Use: A Social and Economic Study* (Farnborough: Gower).

Dixey, R. (1984) 'Women and Leisure', *Modus*, vol. 2(7), pp. 250–2.

Dixey, R. with Talbot, M. (1982) *Women, Leisure and Bingo* (Horsforth, Leeds: Trinity and All Saints College).

Dobbin, I. (1980) *Retirement and Leisure: A Preliminary Research Report*, Centre for Leisure Studies: Salford University.

Dobbs, I. M. and Hill, M. B. (1984) 'Technical Innovation and the Demand for Goods', *Scottish Journal of Political Economy*, vol. 31(2), pp. 147–56.

Douie, V. (c.1945) *The Lesser Half: A Survey of the Laws, Regulations and Practices Introduced During the Present War Which Embody Discrimination Against Women* (London: Women's Publicity Planning Association).

Dumazedier, J. (1960) 'Current Problems in the Sociology of Leisure', *International Social Science Journal*, vol. 2, 4, pp. 522–31.

Duelli-Klein, R. (1983) 'How To Do What We Want To Do: Thoughts About Feminist Methodology', in Bowles, G., Deulli-Klein, R. (eds) *Theories of Women's Studies* (London: Routledge & Kegan Paul).

Dunleavy, P. (1979) 'The Urban Bases of Political Alignment', *British Journal of Political Science*, vol. 19, pp. 409–43.

Dunleavy, P. (1980a) *Urban Political Analysis* (London: Macmillan).

Dunleavy, P. (1980b) 'The Political Implications of Sectoral Cleavages and the Growth of State Employment', *Political Studies*, vol. 28, pp. 364–83 and 527–49.

Dunleavy, P. (1986) The Growth of Sectoral Cleavages and the Stabilisation of State Expenditure, Environment and Planning D, *Society and Space*, vol. 4, pp. 129–44.

Edgell, S. and Duke, V. (1983) 'Gender and Social Policy:The Impact of the Public Expenditure Cuts and Reactions to Them', *Journal of Social Policy*, vol. 12, pp. 357–78.

Ehrenreich, B. and English, D. (1979) *For Her Own Good: 150 Years of the Experts' Advice to Women* (London: Pluto).

Eisenstein, H. (1984) *Contemporary Feminist Thought* (London: Allan & Unwin).

Elliott, B. and McCrone, D. (1981) 'Power and Protest in the City', in Harloe, M. (ed.) *New Perspectives on Urban Change and Conflict* (London: Heinemann).

Elshtain, J. B. (1981) *Public Man, Private Woman. Woman in Social and Political Thought* (Oxford: Martin Robertson).

Equal Opportunities Commission (1983) *Eighth Annual Report* (London: HMSO).

Family Planning Information Service (undated) *Fact Sheet 15* (London: Family Planning Association).

Ferguson, A. (1976) 'Local Variation in Female Workforce Participation Rates and Unemployment Trends', in Burnett, P. (ed.) *Women in Society: A New Perspective*, mimeo.

Ferguson, S. and Fitzgerald, H. (1954) *Social Services UK History of the Second World War* (London: HMSO).

Finch, J. (1983) *Married to the Job: Wives Incorporation in Men's Work* (London: Allen & Unwin).

Foord, J., McDowell, L. and Bowlby, S. (1986) 'For Love Not Money: Gender Relations in Local Areas', *Centre for Urban & Regional Development Studies, Discussion paper 27* (Newcastle Upon Tyne: The University).

Foord, J. and Gregson, N. (1986) 'Patriarchy: Towards a Reconceptualisation', *Antipode*, vol. 18(2), pp. 186–211.

Fox, M. B. (1983) 'Working Women and Travel: The Access of Women to Work and Commuting Facilities', *Journal of the American Planning Association*, vol. 49(2), pp. 165–83.

Frankenberg, R. (1976) 'In the Production of Their Lives. Men (?) . . . Sex and Gender in British Community Studies', in Baker, D. L. and Allen, S. (eds) *Sexual Divisions and Society: Process and Change* (London: Tavistock).

Friedland, R., Piven, F. F. and Alford, R. R. (1977) 'Political Conflict, Urban Structure and the Fiscal Crisis', *International Journal of Urban and Regional Research*, vol. 1, pp. 447–71.

Fyvel, T. R. (1963) *The Insecure Offenders* (London: Chato & Windus).

Gamarnikow, E. and Purvis, J. (1983) 'Introduction', in Gamarnikow, E., Morgan, D., Purvis, J. and Taylorson, D. (eds) *The Public and the Private* (London: Heinemann).

Gamarnikow, E., Morgan, D., Purvis, J. and Taylorson, D. (eds) (1983) *The Public and the Private* (London: Heinemann).

Gavron, H. (1966) *The Captive Wife* (Harmondsworth: Penguin).

Gershuny, J. I. (1982) 'Changing Use of Time in the United Kingdom: 1937–1975, the Self-services Era', *Studies of Broadcasting*, vol. 1, pp. 7–13.

Gershuny, J. I. and Thomas, G. S. (1983) *Changing Times* (Oxford: Oxford University Press).

Goody, J. (1961) Religion and Ritual, *British Journal of Sociology*, vol. XII, pp. 142–64.

Goss, S. (1984) 'Women's Initiatives in Local Government', in Boddy, M. and Fudge, C. (eds) *Local Socialism?* (London: Macmillan).

Greater London Council (1984–7) *Women on the Move* (A series of ten reports) (London: London Strategic Policy Unit).

Greater London Council (1985) *Women and Transport – a Need for a Change*, Proceedings of GLC Women's Committee Conference, October.

Greater London Council (1986) *Changing Places: Positive Action on Women and Planning* (London: GLC).

Gregory, S. (1982) 'Women Among Others: Another View', *Leisure Studies*, vol. 1(1), pp. 47–52.

The Guardian (1981) 'Soap Box Libertarians', 21 April 1981.

The Guardian (1982) Untitled article, 15 September, p. 2.

Guy, C. (1982) 'Push-button Shopping and Retail Development', *Papers in Planning Research, No. 49, Dept. of Town Planning* (Cardiff: UWIST).

Habermas, J. (1976) *Legitimation Crisis* (London: Heinemann).

Hagerstrand, T. (1970) 'What About People in Regional Science', *Papers of the Regional Science Association*, vol. 24, pp. 7–21.

Hall, C. (1982) 'The Butcher, the Baker, the Candlestickmaker: The Shop and the Family in the Industrial Revolution', in Whitelegg *et al.* (eds) *The Changing Experience of Women*, (Oxford/Milton Keynes: Martin Robertson, in association with the Open University).

Hall, J. (1976) 'Subjective Measures of Quality of Life in Britain: 1971 to 1975: Some Developments and Trends', *Social Trends*, vol. 7, pp. 47–60.

Hamilton, R. and Barrett, M. (eds) (1986) *The Politics of Diversity: Feminism, Marxism and Nationalism* (London: Verso).

Hanson, S. and Hanson, P. (1976) *The Daily Activity Patterns of Working Women and Men: Are They Different?* Paper presented to the Annual Meeting of the Association of American Geographers, Milwaukee.

Hanson, S. and Hanson, P. (1980) 'Gender and Urban Activity Patterns in Uppsala, Sweden', *Geographical Review*, vol. 70, pp. 291–9.

Hanson, P. and Hanson, S. (1981) 'The Impact of Married Women's Employment on Household Travel Patterns: A Swedish Example', *Transportation (Amsterdam)*, vol. 10(2), pp. 156–70.

Hanson, S. and Monk, J. (1982) 'On Not Excluding Half the Human in Geography', *Professional Geographer*, vol. 34(1), pp. 11–23.

Harloe, M. (1977) 'Introduction' to Harloe, M. (ed.) *Captive Cities* (London: John Wiley).

Harloe, M. (1981) (ed.) *New Perspectives in Urban Change and Conflict* (London: Heinemann).

Harloe, M. and Lebas, E. (eds) (1981) *City, Class and Capital* (London: Edward Arnold).

Harris, C. (1976) 'Comment on Willmott', in Buxton, M. and Craven, E. (eds) *The Uncertain Future: Demographic Change and Social Policy* (London: Centre for Studies in Social Policy).

Harrison, P. (1975) 'The Gambling Class', *New Society*, no. 650, 20 March, pp. 720–2.

Hartnett, O. (1978) 'Sex Role Stereotyping and Work', in Chetwynd, J. and Hartnett, O. (eds) *The Sex Role System* (London: Routledge & Kegan Paul).

Harvey, D. (1974) *Social Justice and the City* (London: Edward Arnold).

Hayden, D. (1982) *The Grand Domestic Revolution* (Massachusetts: MIT Press).

Hayford, A. (1974) 'The Geography of Women: An Historical Introduction', *Antipode*, vol. 6(2), pp. 1–19.

Helms, J. (1974) 'Old Women in America: The Need for Social Justice', *Antipode*, vol. 6(3), pp. 26–33.

Hemmens, G. G., (1970) 'Analysis and Simulation of Urban Activity Patterns', *Socio-Economic Planning Sciences*, vol. 4, pp. 53–66.

Hillman, M. (1970) *Mobility in New towns*. Unpublished Ph.D. thesis, University of Edinburgh.

Hillman, M., Henderson, I. and Whalley, A. (1973) *Personal Mobility and Transport Policy*, Broadsheet 542 (London: Political and Economic Planning).

Hillman, M., Henderson, I. and Whalley, A. (1974) *Mobility and Accessibility in the Outer Metropolitan Area. Political and Economic Planning*, Report to the Department of the Environment (London: Policy Studies Institute).

Hillman, M., Henderson, I. and Whalley, A. (1976) *Transport Realities and Planning Policy* (London: Political and Economic Planning).

Hillman, M. and Whalley, A. (1972) *Fair Play for All, A Study of Access to Sport and Informal Recreation* (London: Political and Economic Planning).

The Independent Commission on Transport (1974) *Changing Directions* (London: Coronet Books).

Institute of Grocery Distribution (1980) *Developments in the Grocery Trade*, An IGD presentation at Reading University (London: IGD).

International Publishing Corporation (1970) *Shopping in the Seventies* IPC Women's Weekly Group, British Market Research Bureau Ltd, Saunders House, 53 The Mall, London W5.

Imray, and Middleton (1983) 'Public and Private: Marking the Boundaries', in Gamarnikow, E., Morgan, E., Purvis, J. and Taylorson, D. (eds) *The Public and The Private* (London: Heinemann).

Jackson, B. and Jackson, S. (1979) *Childminder: A Study in Action Research* (Harmondsworth: Penguin).

Jeffreys, J. B. (1954) *Retail Trading in Britain, 1850–1950* (Cambridge: Cambridge University Press).

Jones, P., Clarke, M. I., Dix, M. C. and Heggie, I. (1983) *Understanding Travel Behaviour* (Farnborough: Gower).

Jones, T. S. M. (1977) *Young Children and Their School Journey: A Survey in Oxfordshire*, Dept of the Environment, and Dept of Transport. TRRL Report SR 342 (Crowthorne: Transport and Road Research Laboratory).

Joseph, G. (1983) *Women at Work* (Oxford: Phillip Allan).

Keeble, L. (1952) *Principles and Practice of Town and Country Planning* (London: Estates Gazette).

Kirby, D. A. (1982) 'Shopping and the Micro-chip', *Town and Country Planning*, vol. 51, January, pp. 10–13.

Klausner, D. (1986) 'Beyond Separate Spheres: Linking Production With Social Reproduction and Consumption', *Society and Space*, vol. 4, pp. 29–41.

Klodawsky, F., Aron, S. and Rose, D. (1985) *Single Parent Families and Canadian House Policy: How Mothers Lose* (Ottawa: Canadian Mortgage and Housing Corporation).

Kuper, L. (ed.) (1953) *Living in Towns* (London: Crescent Press).

Labour Party (1981) *Listen to Women for a Change* (London: The Labour Party).

Leathard, A. (1980) *The Fight for Family Planning: The Development of Family Planning Services in Britain 1921–74* (London: Macmillan).

Lebas, E. (1977) 'Regional Policy Research: Some Theoretical and Methodological Problems', in Harloe, M. (ed.) *Captive Cities* (London: John Wiley).

Lenntorp, B. (1979) 'A Time-geographic Simulation Model of Individual Activity Programmes', in Carlstein, T., Parkes, D. N. and Thrift, N. J. (eds) *Timing Space and Spacing Time in Socio-economic Systems* (London: Edward Arnold).

Levin, P. H. and Bruce, J. A. (1967) *The Location of Primary Schools*. Note ED 71/67 (Garston: Ministry of Public Buildings and Works, Building Research Station).

Lewis, J. (1984) 'The Role of Female Employment in the Industrial Restructuring and Regional Development of the United Kingdom', *Antipode*, vol. 16(4), pp. 47–59.

Lewis, J. (1985) 'Technical Change in Retailing: Its Impact on Employment and Access', *Environment and Planning B: Planning and Design*, vol. 12, pp. 165–91.

Ley, D. (1980) 'Liberal Ideology and the Post Industrial City', *Annals of the Association of American Geographers*, vol. 70, pp. 238–58.

Libbee, M. and McGee, D. (1979) *Spatial Analysis of Some Factors Related to the Women's Movement*. Paper presented at Annual Meeting of the Association of American Geographers.

Lojkine, J. (1976) 'Contribution to a Marxist Theory of Capitalist

Urbanisation', in Pickvance C. (ed.) *Urban Society: Critical Essays* (London: Methuen).

Lojkine, J. (1977) 'Big Firms, Strategies, Urban Policy and Urban Social Movements', in Harloe, M. (ed.) *Captive Cities* (London: John Wiley).

Lloyd, B. (1978) 'The Quiet Revolution in Geography', *Union of Socialist Geographers Newsletters* No. 3, pp. 30–2.

Luxton, M. (1980) *More Than a Labour of Love: Three Generations of Women's Work in the Home* (Toronto: Women's Press).

Mackie, L. and Patullo, P. (1977) *Women at Work* (London: Tavistock Press).

McClelland, W. G. (1962) 'The Supermarket and Society', *Sociological Review*, NS, vol. 10, pp. 133–44.

McClelland, W. G. (1963) *Studies in Retailing* (Oxford: Basil Blackwell).

McDowell, L. (1979) 'Women in British Geography', *Area*, vol. 11, pp. 151–4.

McDowell, L. (1981) *Capitalism, Patriarchy and the Sexual Division of Space*. Paper presented to the Conference on the Institutionalisation of Sex Differences (Canterbury: University of Kent).

McDowell, L. (1982) 'City and Home: Urban Housing and the Sexual Division of Space', in Evans, M. and Ungerson, C. (eds) *Sexual Divisions, Patterns and Processes* (Andover: Tavistock).

McDowell, L. (1983) 'Towards an Understanding of the Gender Division of Urban Space', *Environment and Planning D: Society and Space*, vol. 1, pp. 59–72.

McDowell, L. and Bowlby, S. R. (1983) 'Teaching Feminist Geography', *Journal of Geography in Higher Education*, vol. 7(2), pp. 97–107.

McGoldrick, P. J. (1984) 'Trends in Retailing and Consumer Behaviour', in Davies, R. L. and Rogers, D. S. (eds) *Store Location and Store Assessment Research* (Chichester: John Wiley).

Mackenzie, S. (1979) Mimeo (utitled), University of Sussex.

Mackenzie, S. (1980) 'Women and the Reproduction of Labour Power in the Industrial City: A Case Study', *Urban and Regional Studies, Working Paper 23* (Brighton: University of Sussex).

Mackenzie, S. (1983) *Gender and Environment: Reproduction of Labour in Post War Brighton*, D.Phil Thesis, University of Sussex.

Mackenzie, S. (1984) Editorial Introduction, *Antipode*, vol. 16(3), p. 10.

Mackenzie, S. (1986) *Women and Canadian Geography*, A paper presented to the Annual Meeting of the Institute of British Geographers, Reading, England.

Mackenzie, S. (1988) 'Restructuring the Relations of Work and Life: Women as Environmental Actors, Feminism as Geographic Analysis', in Kobayashi, A. and Mackenzie, S. (eds) *Humanism and Historical Materialism in Geography* (London: Hutchinson).

Mackenzie, S. and Rose, D. (1982) 'On the Necessity for Feminist Scholarship in Human Geography', *The Professional Geographer*, vol. 34(2), pp. 220–3.

Mackenzie, S. and Rose, D. (1983) 'Industrial Change, the Domestic Economy and Home Life', in Anderson, J., Duncan, S. and Hudson, R.

(eds) *Redundant Spaces? Social Change and Industrial Decline in Cities and Regions* (London: Academic Press).

Madden, J. F. (1977) 'A Spatial Theory of Sex Discrimination', *Journal of Regional Science*, vol. 17, pp. 369–80.

Mama, A. (1984) 'Black Women: The Economic Crisis and the British State', *Feminist Review*, vol. 17, pp. 21–35.

Markusen, A. (1980) 'City Spatial Structure, Women's Household Work, and National Urban Policy', in Stimpson, C. *et al.* (eds) *Women and the American City* (Chicago: University of Chicago Press).

Marshall, K. (1982) *Real Freedom* (London: Junius).

Martin, J. and Roberts, C. (1984) *Women and Employment: A Lifetime Perspective*, Department of Employment and OPCS (London: HMSO).

Massey, D. (1984a) *Spatial Divisions of Labour* (London: Macmillan).

Massey, D. (1984b) 'Introduction', in Massey, D. and Allen J. (eds) *Geography Matters!* (Milton Keynes/Cambridge: The Open University/ Cambridge University Press).

Matrix (1984) *Making Space: Women and the Man-made Environment* (London: Pluto).

Mayo, M. (ed.) (1977) *Women in the Community* (London: Routledge & Kegan Paul).

Mies, M. (1979) 'Towards a Methodology of Womens' Studies', *Institute of Social Studies Occasional Papers, No. 77* (The Hague: Institute of Social Studies).

Miller, R. (1982) 'Household Activity Patterns in Nineteenth-Century Suburbs: A Time-Geographic Exploration', *Annals of the Association of American Geographers*, vol. 72, pp. 355–71.

Miller, R. (1983) 'The Hoover in the Garden: Middle Class Women and Suburbanization, 1850–1920', *Environment and Planning D, Society and Space,* vol. 1(1), pp. 73–87.

Mingione, E. (1977) 'Theoretical Elements for a Marxist Analysis of Urban Development', in Harloe, M. (ed.) *Captive Cities* (London: John Wiley).

Ministry of Transport (1965) *Highway Statistics* (London: HMSO).

Mitchell, J. (1971) *Womens Estate* (Harmondsworth: Penguin).

Momsen, J. and Townsend, J. (eds) (1987) *The Geography of Gender in the Third World* (London: Hutchinson).

Murcott, A. (1983) *Eat Up, It's Good for You: Essays on the Sociological Significance of Food* (Aldershot: Gower).

Myrdal, A. and Klein, V. (1956 and 1968) *Women's Two Roles* (London: Routledge & Kegan Paul).

Nadel, S. F. (1954) *Nupe Religion* (London: Cohen & West).

National Campaign for Nursery Education (n.d. *c.* 1980) *Fact Sheet* (London: NCNE).

National Campaign for Nursery Education (1981) *Nursery Education under Attack* (London: NCNE).

National Child Care Campaign (1981) *Nurseries: How and Why to Fight for Them* (London: NCCC).

National Childminders Association (1969) *Who cares?*, Spring issue.

North Tyneside Community Development Project (1978) *North Shields: Women's Work*, Final Report 5 (London: HMSO).

Oakley, A. (1974) *Housewife* (London: Allen Lane).

Oakley, A. (1976) *Women's Work: The Housewife, Past and Present* (New York: Vintage).

The Observer (1982) Untitled article, 4 July, p. 25.

Office of Population Censuses and Surveys (1952) *Economic Activity Tables*, Census of Population (London: HMSO).

Office of Population Censuses and Surveys (1978) *The General Household Survey 1976* (London: HMSO).

Office of Population Censuses and Surveys (1981) *Economic Activity Tables*, Census of Population (London: HMSO).

Office of Population Censuses and Surveys (1982a) *Labour Force Survey 1981* (London: HMSO).

Office of Population Censuses and Surveys (1982b) *OPCS Monitor* 1981 Census, Monitor Reference CEN81CM57 (London: HMSO).

Office of Population Censuses and Surveys (1984) *Population Trends*, 37.6.14 (London: HMSO).

Osborn, A. F. (1983) 'Material Employment, Depression and Child Behaviour', *EQC Research Bulletin*, vol. 8, pp. 48–67.

Pahl, J. M. and Pahl, R. E. (1971) *Managers and Their Wives* (Harmondsworth: Penguin).

Pahl, R. E. (1971) 'Poverty and the Urban System', in Chisholm, M. and Manners, G. (eds) *Spatial Policy Problems of the British Economy* (London: Cambridge University Press).

Pahl, R. (1975) *Whose City?* (Harmondsworth: Penguin).

Pahl, R. E. (1977a) 'Collective Consumption and the State in Capitalist and State Socialist Societies', in Scase, R. (ed.) *Industrial Society: Class, Cleavage and Control* (London: Tavistock).

Pahl, R. E. (1977b) 'Managers, Technical Experts and the State', in M. Harloe (ed.) *Captive Cities* (London: John Wiley).

Pahl, R. E. (1984) *Divisions of Labour* (Oxford: Basil Blackwell).

Palm, R. (1981) 'Women in Non-metropolitan Areas: A Time Budget Survey', *Environment and Planning A*, vol. 13, pp. 373–8.

Palm, R. and Pred, A. (1974) *A Time Geographic Perspective on Problems of Inequality for Women*. Working paper 236 (Berkeley: Institute of Urban and Regional Development, University of California).

Parker, S. (1976) *The Sociology of Leisure* (London: Allen & Unwin).

Peake, L. (1985) 'Teaching Feminist Geography: Another Perspective', *Journal of Geography in Higher Education*, vol. 9(2), pp. 186–90.

Peet, R. (1975) 'Inequality and Poverty: A Marxist-Geographic Theory', *Annals of the Association of American Geographers*, vol. 65(4), pp. 564–71.

Phillips, A. (1983) *Hidden Hands* (London: Pluto Press).

Phillips, A. (1987) *Divided Loyalties: Dilemmas of Sex and Class* (London: Virago).

Pickup, L. (1981) *Housewives' Mobility and Travel Patterns*. Dept of the Environment and Dept of Transport, TRRL, Report LR 971 (Crowthorne: Transport and Road Research Laboratory).

Pickup, L. (1983) *Travel Issues in Women's Job Choice: An Activity Based*

Approach. Unpublished PhD thesis, Department of Geography, Reading University.

Pickup, L. and Town, S. W. (1981) *The Role of Social Science Methodologies in Transport Planning*. TRRL Supplementary Report, SR 698 (Crowthorne: Transport and Road Research Laboratory).

Pickup, L. and Town, S. W. (1983) *A European Study of Commuting and Its Consequences*. European Foundation for the Improvement of Living and Working Conditions Report (Shankhill, Co. Dublin: European Foundation).

Pickvance, C. (ed.) (1976) *Urban Society: Critical Essays* (London: Methuen).

Pike, B. (1984) 'Safe Women's Transport', in Bruce, A. and Hedley R. (eds) *Needs Based Transport Planning, New Directions in Public and Community Provision* (London: Camden Needs Based Transport Planning Group).

Pinchbeck, I. (1969) *Women Workers and the Industrial Revolution 1750–1850* (London: Frank Cass; first published 1930).

Pirie, G. H. (1976) 'Thoughts on Revealed Preference and Spatial Behaviour', *Environment and Planning*, A, vol. 8, pp. 947–55.

Pre-school Playgroups Association (1978) *Report on Parental Involvement in Playgroups* (London: PPA).

Pre-school Playgroups Association (1980) *PPA Coming of Age in the Eighties: Thoughts of the President and Vice Presidents* (London: PPA).

Preteceille, E. (1981) 'Collective Consumption, the State and the Crisis of Capitalist Society', in Harloe, M. and Lebas, E. (ed.) *City, Class and Capital* (London: Edward Arnold).

Preteceille, E. (1986) 'Collective Consumption, Urban Segregation and Social Classes', *Society and Space*, vol. 4, pp. 145–54.

Radio Times (1982) Untitled article, 11 September, p. 42.

Randall, V. (1982) *Women and Politics* (London: Macmillan).

Reddaway, W. B. (1939) *The Economics of Declining Population* (London: Allen & Unwin).

Rengert, G. (1975) 'Some Effects of Being Female on Criminal Spatial Behaviour', *The Pennsylvania Geographer*, vol. 13(2), pp. 10–18.

Reynolds, J. (1983) *Retail Employment Change in Tyne and Wear*, CURDS (Newcastle upon Tyne: The University).

Rich, D. (1953) 'Spare Time in the Black Country', in Kuper, L. (ed.) *Living in Towns* (London: Crescent Press).

Riley, D. (1979) 'War in the Nursery', *Feminist Review*, vol. 2, pp. 82–108.

Roberts, E. (1982) 'Working Wives and Their Families', in Barker, T. and Drake, M. (eds) *Population and Society in Britain 1850–1980* (London: Batsford).

Roberts, H. (1986) 'After Sixteen: What Choice', in Burgess, R. G. (ed.) *Exploring Society* (London: Longman).

Rogers, B. (1983) *52% Getting Women's Power into Politics* (London: The Women's Press).

Rojeck, C. (1985) *Capitalism and Leisure Theory* (Andover: Tavistock).

Rowe, K. (1977) *Nursery Education and Equal Opportunities for Women*, National Campaign for Nursery Education, mimeo.

Rubin, G. (1975) 'Comment: Prostitution in Nevada', *Annals of the Association of American Geographers*, vol. 65, pp. 115–18.

Rushton, G. (1969) 'Analysis of Spatial Behaviour by Revealed Space Preferences', *Annals of the Association of American Geographers*, vol. 59, pp. 391–400.

Saunders, P. (1979) *Urban Politics: A Sociological Interpretaton* (London: Hutchinson).

Saunders, P. (1981) *Social Theory and the Urban Question* (London: Hutchinson).

Schlesinger, G. (1982) 'Working Women's Travel Issues', *Transportation Research Forum Annual Meeting*, vol. 23(1), pp. 436–42.

Scott, R. (1976) *The Female Consumer* (London: Associated Business Press).

Scott, J. and Tilly, L. (1975) 'Women's Work and the Family in Nineteeth Century Europe', in Rosenberg, C. E. (ed.) *Family History* (Pennsylvania: University of Pennsylvania Press).

Segal, L. (1987) *Is the Future Female? Troubled Thoughts on Contemporary Feminism* (London: Virago).

Siltanen, J. and Stanworth, M. (1984) 'The Politics of Private Woman and Public Man', in Siltanen, J. and Stanworth, M. (eds) *Women and the Public Sphere* (London: Hutchinson).

Sofer, C. (1965) 'Buying and Selling: A Study in the Sociology of Distribution', *Sociological Review*, vol. 13, pp. 183–309.

Soja, E. (1971) 'The Political Organisation of Space', *Commission of College Geography Resource Paper, No. 8* (Washington DC: Association of American Geographers).

Spárks, L. (1984) *The Impact of the Recession on Retail Employment*. Paper presented at the IBG Annual Conference, Durham University, January.

Spender, D. (1982) *Women of Ideas and What Men have Done to Them: From Appra Benn to Adrienne Rich* (London: Routledge & Kegan Paul).

Spring Rice, M. (1981) *Working Class Wives: Their Health and Conditions* (London: Virago).

Stacey, M. and Price, M. (1981) *Women, Power and Politics* (Andover, Tavistock).

Stanley, L. and Wise, L. (1983) 'Back into the Personal or: Our Attempt to Construct Feminist Research', in Bowles, G. and Duelli-Klein, R. (eds) *Theories of Women's Studies* (London: Routledge & Kegan Paul).

Stanworth, M. (1987) *Reproductive Technologies* (Oxford: Polity Press).

Stapleton-Concorde, C. (1986) *A Geography for Women Who Are Homeless in America*', Paper presented at the Annual Conference of the Association of American Geographers.

Stimpson, C., Dixler, E., Nelson, M. and Yatrakis, K. (eds) (1981) *Women and the American City* (Chicago: University of Chicago Press).

Sullivan, D. G. (1981) 'How Tele-shopping Will Change Marketing', *Marketing Times*, vol. 28, pp. 1.

Talbot, M. (1979) *Women and Leisure: A State of Art Review*, SRC/Sports Council Joint Panel on Sport and Leisure Research, London.

Tanburn, J. (1968) *Food, Women and Shops*, Lintas Special Projects (London: Lintas).

Tanner, J. C. (1983) *International Comparisons of Cars and Car Usage*. TRRL Laboratory Report, LR1070 (Crowthorne: Transport and Road Research Laboratory).

Thompson, B. and Finlayson, A. (1963) 'Married Women Who Work in Early Motherhood', *British Journal of Sociology*, vol. 14, pp. 150–68.

Thorns, D. C. (1972) *Suburbia* (London: MacGibbon & Kee).

Thrift, N. (1976) 'An Introduction to Time Geography', *Catmog No. 13*, University of East Anglia: Geo Abstracts Ltd.

Thrift, N. and Pred, A. (1981) 'Time-geography: A New Beginning', *Progress in Human Geography*, vol. 5, pp. 277–86.

Tilly, L. and Scott, J. (1978) *Women, Work and Family* (New York: Rinehart & Winston).

Titmuss, R. and Titmuss, K. (1942) *Parents Revolt: A Study of the Declining Birth Rate in Acquisitive Societies* (London: Secker & Warburg).

Titmuss, R. M. (1968) *Commitment to Welfare* (London: Allen & Unwin).

Tivers, J. (1977) 'Constraints on Spatial Activity Patterns – Women with Young Children', *Department of Geography Occasional paper in Geography, No. 6* (London: Kings College).

Tivers, J. (1978) 'How the Other Half Lives: An Historical Study of Women', *Area*, vol. 10, 4, pp. 302–6.

Tivers, J. (1985) *Women Attached: The Daily Lives of Women with Young Children* (London: Croom-Helm).

Tizard, J., Moss, P. and Perry, J. (1976) *All Our Children: Pre-school Services in a Changing Society* (London: Temple Smith/New Society).

Trades Union Congress (1980) *Women Workers*, 1980: Report for 1979–80 of the TUC Women's Advisory Committee and Report of the 50th TUC Women's Conference (London: TUC).

Troyna, B. and Smith, D. (1983) (eds) *Racism, School and The Labour Market* (Leicester: National Youth Bureau).

Ungerson, C. (1981) *Women and Caring – Material and Ideological Determinants. The Institutionalisation of Gender Differences*. Institute of British Geographers Annual Conference, Southampton University.

Unit for Retail Planing and Information (1984) *List of U.K. Hypermarkets and Superstores* (Reading: URPI).

Urry, J. (1981) 'Localities, Regions and the Social Class', *International Journal of Urban and Regional Research*, vol. 5, pp. 455–74.

Walby, S. (1983) *Women's Unemployment: Some Spatial and Historical Variants*. Paper presented at the Urban Change and Conflict Conference, Clacton, England.

Wekerle, G. R. (1984) 'A Woman's Place Is in the City', *Antipode*, 16(3) pp. 11–19.

Wekerle, G., Peterson, R. and Morley, D. (eds) (1980) *New Space for Women* (Boulder, Col.: Westview).

White, C. L. (1970) *Women's Magazines 1963–1968* (London: Michael Joseph).

Willis, P. (1978) *Learning to Labour* (Farnborough: Saxon House).

Wilson, E. (1977a) *Women and the Welfare State* (Andover: Tavistock).

Wilson, E. (1977b) 'Women in the Community', in Mayo, M. (ed.) *Women in the Community* (Routledge & Kegan Paul).

Wilson, E. (1980) *Only Halfway to Paradise* (Andover: Tavistock).

Women and Geography Study Group of the Institute of British Geographers (1984) *Geography and Gender: An Introduction to Feminist Geography* (London: Hutchinson and Explorations in Feminism Collective).

Women's Equality Group (1987) *London Women in the 1980s* (London: Strategic Policy Group).

Women's Groups on Public Welfare Hygiene Committee (1943) *Our Towns: A Closeup* (London: Oxford University Press).

Woods, K. (1982) *Studies Affecting Carsharing for Journeys to Work*. TRRL Supplementary Report (Crowthorne: Transport and Road Research Laboratory).

Young, M. and Willmott, P. (1973) *The Symmetrical family* (Harmondsworth: Penguin).

Zelinsky, W., Monk, J. and Hanson, S. (1982) 'Women and Geography: A Review and Prospectus', *Progress in Human Geography*, vol. 6(3), pp. 317–66.

Index